W

LEARN ENGLISH

through
CLASSIC LITERATURE:

American Tales of
HORROR
and the
SUPERNATURAL

KAPLAN
PUBLISHING
New York • Chicago

Look for these other Kaplan books:

Learn English through Classic Literature: The Short Stories and Essays of Mark Twain

TOEFL Idiom Flashcards

TOEFL Vocabulary Flashcards

LEARN ENGLISH

through

CLASSIC LITERATURE:

American Tales of Horror
and the Supernatural

KAPLAN)

PUBLISHING

New York • Chicago

Editorial Director: Jennifer Farthing
Senior Editor: Ruth Baygell
Production Editor: Karen Goodfriend
Production Artist: Ellen Gurak
Cover Designer: Carly Schnur

Published by Kaplan Publishing, a division of Kaplan, Inc.
888 Seventh Ave.
New York, NY 10106

November 2006
10 9 8 7 6 5 4 3 2 1

ISBN-13: 978-1-4195-4218-3
ISBN-10: 1-4195-4218-4

Table of Contents

How to Use This Book

This book contains stories that fall under the category of classic American horror and the supernatural. It defines over 700 words and idioms, part of the core vocabulary of English, including both formal written terms you are likely to encounter in university-level texts and informal spoken language.

The stories and essays are printed on the right-hand pages, with key TOEFL vocabulary terms given in bold type. Definitions for these key terms are given on the left-hand page, facing the text, along with grammatical information about the term's part of speech (whether it is a noun, verb, adjective, etc.).

While the texts have not been simplified or shortened, slight changes have been made in a few cases for ease of understanding.

Read this book in order.

Most of the words are defined the first time they appear, so if you pay close attention to the defined words on each page, you will reinforce your knowledge when you see them again later on in the book. Each time the word appears again, it will be a test of your new TOEFL vocabulary knowledge.

Give yourself mini-quizzes to review.

Each page of the book contains a manageable number of vocabulary terms. Since the terms appear in bold on the right-hand page without definitions, you can use each page like a flashcard to quiz yourself: Read through the page, checking the TOEFL vocabulary words as you go to make sure you know them. Then, when you get to the end of the page, go back and test your memory by looking at the bold terms in the text. Try to remember what they mean, and then check the left-hand page to see if you are right.

Develop a list of difficult words to work on.

When you finish an entire story or essay, go back through the word lists again, using the mini-quiz technique. You will surely have remembered more of these key words than you did the first time, but there will probably be a few that you continue to have trouble with. Keep your own list of challenging words, and work on it when possible.

Learning a new word in context of its meaning is more effective (and a lot more fun) than memorizing it from a list. Good luck!

sensible *(adjective)* reasonable, having good
  sense

remark *(noun)* comment

plunge[d] *(verb)* to throw forcefully into a
  substance or place

Story of the Vanishing Patient

by Elia Wilkinson Peattie

There had always been strange stories about the house, but it was a **sensible,** comfortable sort of a neighborhood, and people took pains to say to one another that there was nothing in these tales—of course not! Absolutely nothing! How could there be? It was a matter of common **remark,** however, that considering the amount of money the Nethertons had spent on the place, it was curious they lived there so little. They were nearly always away,—up North in the summer and down South in the winter, and over to Paris or London now and then,—and when they did come home it was only to entertain a number of guests from the city. The place was either **plunged** in gloom or gayety. The old gardener who kept house by himself in the cottage at the back of the yard had things much his own way by far the greater part of the time.

absurd *(adjective)* not typical
benefit *(noun)* advantage; help
silvered *(adjective)* having a silver color

masses *(noun)* groups of

speculate[d] *(verb)* to wonder or think
impalpably *(adverb)* not able to be touched
undeniably *(adverb)* not able to deny or
    contradict

worn out *(idiom)* used up; too tired

Dr. Block and his wife lived next door to the Nethertons, and he and his wife, who were so **absurd** as to be very happy in each other's company, had the **benefit** of the beautiful yard. They walked there mornings when the leaves were **silvered** with dew, and evenings they sat beside the lily pond and listened for the whip-poor-will. The doctor's wife moved her room over to that side of the house which commanded a view of the yard, and thus made the honeysuckles and laurel and clematis and all the **masses** of tossing greenery her own. Sitting there day after day with her sewing, she **speculated** about the mystery which hung **impalpably** yet **undeniably** over the house.

It happened one night when she and her husband had gone to their room, and were congratulating themselves on the fact that he had no very sick patients and was likely to enjoy a good night's rest, that a ring came at the door.

"If it's any one wanting you to leave home," warned his wife, "you must tell them you are all **worn out.** You've been disturbed every night this week, and it's too much!"

The young physician went downstairs. At the

hasten *(verb)* to hurry

plot *(noun)* plan
has designs on you *(idiom)* to have plans to do
     something to someone
revolver *(noun)* a type of gun

made out *(idiom)* was able to recognize

door stood a man whom he had never seen before.

"My wife is lying very ill next door," said the stranger, "so ill that I fear she will not live till morning. Will you please come to her at once?"

"Next door?" cried the physician. "I didn't know the Nethertons were home!"

"Please **hasten,**" begged the man. "I must go back to her. Follow as quickly as you can."

The doctor went back upstairs to complete his toilet.

"How absurd," protested his wife when she heard the story. "There is no one at the Nethertons'. I sit where I can see the front door, and no one can enter without my knowing it, and I have been sewing by the window all day. If there were any one in the house, the gardener would have the porch lantern lighted. It is some **plot.** Some one **has designs on you.** You must not go."

But he went. As he left the room his wife placed a **revolver** in his pocket.

The great porch of the mansion was dark, but the physician **made out** that the door was open, and he entered. A feeble light came on the bronze

head of [the stairs] *(idiom)* the top of

topped him *(idiom)* was taller than him

flush[ed] *(verb)* to glow
midst *(noun)* the middle point

feeble *(adjective)* weak
appealingly *(adverb)* in a manner to show a
　　desire or request
involuntarily *(adverb)* without meaning to
anguish *(noun)* sadness, pain, or distress

stimulating *(adjective)* increasing excitement

lamp at the turn of the stairs, and by it he found his way, his feet sinking noiselessly in the rich carpets. At the **head of** the stairs the man met him. The doctor thought himself a tall man, but the stranger **topped him** by half a head. He motioned the physician to follow him, and the two went down the hall to the front room. The place was **flushed** with a rose-colored glow from several lamps. On a silken couch, in the **midst** of pillows, lay a woman dying with consumption. She was like a lily, white, shapely, graceful, with **feeble** yet charming movements. She looked at the doctor **appealingly,** then, seeing in his eyes the **involuntary** verdict that her hour was at hand, she turned toward her companion with a glance of **anguish.** Dr. Block asked a few questions. The man answered them, the woman remaining silent. The physician administered something **stimulating,** and then wrote a prescription which he placed on the mantel-shelf.

"The drug store is closed to-night," he said, "and I fear the druggist has gone home. You can have the prescription filled the first thing in the morning, and I will be over before breakfast."

long[ed] *(verb)* to wish or hope for
oblivious *(adjective)* unaware

impassioned *(adjective)* showing a lot of
     emotion
unutterable *(adjective)* not able to be spoken or
     described
temples *(noun)* the flat side of the forehead

voluminous *(adjective)* large and bulky

quiet[ed] *(verb)* to make quiet, silent, or still

considerate *(adjective)* thoughtful of others

After that, there was no reason why he should not have gone home. Yet, oddly enough, he preferred to stay. Nor was it professional anxiety that prompted this delay. He **longed** to watch those mysterious persons, who, almost **oblivious** of his presence, were speaking their mortal farewells in their glances, which were **impassioned** and of **unutterable** sadness.

He sat as if fascinated. He watched the glitter of rings on the woman's long, white hands, he noted the waving of light hair about her **temples**, he observed the details of her gown of soft white silk which fell about her in **voluminous** folds. Now and then the man gave her of the stimulant which the doctor had provided; sometimes he bathed her face with water. Once he paced the floor for a moment till a motion of her hand **quieted** him.

After a time, feeling that it would be more sensible and **considerate** of him to leave, the doctor made his way home. His wife was awake, impatient to hear of his experiences.

She listened to his tale in silence, and when he had finished she turned her face to the wall and made no comment.

dewy *(adjective)* damp with moisture

chanced to be *(idiom)* happened to be; by coincidence

attend *(verb)* to take care of or assist

bid *(verb)* to be asked

"You seem to be ill, my dear," he said. "You have a chill. You are shivering."

"I have no chill," she replied sharply. "But I—well, you may leave the light burning."

The next morning before breakfast the doctor crossed the **dewy** lawn to the Netherton house. The front door was locked, and no one answered to his repeated ringings. The old gardener **chanced to be** cutting the grass near at hand, and he came running up.

"What you ringin' that door-bell for, doctor?" said he. "The folks ain't come home yet. There ain't nobody there."

"Yes, there is, Jim. I was called here last night. A man came for me to **attend** his wife. They must both have fallen asleep that the bell is not answered. I wouldn't be surprised to find her dead, as a matter of fact. She was a desperately sick woman. Perhaps she is dead and something has happened to him. You have the key to the door, Jim. Let me in."

But the old man was shaking in every limb, and refused to do as he was **bid.**

"Don't you never go in there, doctor," whispered

nohow *(adverb)* not for any reason

stipulate[d] *(verb)* to promise; to force to agree

mount[ed] *(verb)* to climb

occupancy *(noun)* the state of being living in or
occupied

vacant *(adjective)* empty; not lived in

musty *(adjective)* smelling old and damp

he, with chattering teeth. "Don't you go for to 'tend no one. You jus' come tell me when you sent for that way. No, I ain't goin' in, doctor, **nohow**. It ain't part of my duties to go in. That's been **stipulated** by Mr. Netherton. It's my business to look after the garden."

Argument was useless. Dr. Block took the bunch of keys from the old man's pocket and himself unlocked the front door and entered. He **mounted** the steps and made his way to the upper room. There was no evidence of **occupancy**. The place was silent, and, so far as living creature went, **vacant**. The dust lay over everything. It covered the delicate fabric of the sofa where he had seen the dying woman. It rested on the pillows. The place smelled **musty** and evil, as if it had not been used for a long time. The lamps of the room held not a drop of oil.

But on the mantel-shelf was the prescription which the doctor had written the night before. He read it, folded it, and put it in his pocket.

As he locked the outside door the old gardener came running to him.

"Don't you never go up there again, will you?" he

plead[ed] *(verb)* to beg; to ask

pleaded, "not unless you see all the Nethertons home and I come for you myself. You won't, doctor?"

"No," said the doctor.

When he told his wife she kissed him, and said: "Next time when I tell you to stay at home, you must stay!"

luminous *(adjective)* giving off light

solitude *(noun)* the state of being alone

arrestment *(noun)* the state of being stopped or suspended

save the *(idiom)* except for

obliterated *(adjective)* completely destroyed

poignant *(adjective)* full of emotion

immeasurable *(adjective)* not able to be measured

vast *(adjective)* massive or large is size and space

billows *(noun)* wave

spaciousness *(noun)* the state of having a large amount of space

On the Northern Ice

by Elia Wilkinson Peattie

The winter nights up at Sault Ste. Marie are as white and **luminous** as the Milky Way. The silence which rests upon the **solitude** appears to be white also. Even sound has been included in Nature's **arrestment,** for, indeed, **save the** still white frost, all things seem to be **obliterated.** The stars have a **poignant** brightness, but they belong to heaven and not to earth, and between their **immeasurable** height and the still ice rolls the ebony ether in **vast,** liquid **billows.**

In such a place it is difficult to believe that the world is actually peopled. It seems as if it might be the dark of the day after Cain killed Abel, and as if all of humanity's remainder was huddled in affright away from the awful **spaciousness** of Creation.

The night Ralph Hagadorn started out for Echo Bay—bent on a pleasant duty—he laughed to

shot away *(idiom)* moved quickly

bent on *(idiom)* determined to do something

tang *(noun)* something that stimulates the senses

keen *(adjective)* sharp

venture *(noun)* risky task

cleaves *(verb)* to split

fancies *(noun)* imaginary thoughts

hasten[ing] *(verb)* to hurry

auspicious *(adjective)* fortunate; favorable

himself, and said that he did not at all object to being the only man in the world, so long as the world remained as unspeakably beautiful as it was when he buckled on his skates and **shot away** into the solitude. He was **bent on** reaching his best friend in time to act as groomsman, and business had delayed him till time was at its briefest. So he journeyed by night and journeyed alone, and when the **tang** of the frost got at his blood, he felt as a spirited horse feels when it gets free of bit and bridle. The ice was as glass, his skates were **keen,** his frame fit, and his **venture** to his taste! So he laughed, and cut through the air as a sharp stone **cleaves** the water. He could hear the whistling of the air as he cleft it.

As he went on and on in the black stillness, he began to have **fancies.** He imagined himself enormously tall—a great Viking of the Northland, **hastening** over icy fiords to his love. And that reminded him that he had a love—though, indeed, that thought was always present with him as a background for other thoughts. To be sure, he had not told her that she was his love, for he had seen her only a few times, and the **auspicious** occa-

swiftly *(adverb)* in a quick manner

exultation *(noun)* happiness; joy

expectancy *(noun)* the state of expecting
   something

about her [throat] *(idiom)* around her

scourge[d] *(verb)* to punish

chagrin *(noun)* frustration from distress or
   being humiliated

temerity *(noun)* a lack of consideration for
   danger

determination *(noun)* the result of settling a
   question

sion had not yet presented itself. She lived at Echo
Bay also, and was to be the maid of honor to his
friend's bride—which was one more reason why
he skated almost as **swiftly** as the wind, and why,
now and then, he let out a shout of **exultation.**

The one cloud that crossed Hagadorn's sun
of **expectancy** was the knowledge that Marie
Beaujeu's father had money, and that Marie lived in
a house with two stories to it, and wore otter skin
about her throat and little satin-lined mink boots
on her feet when she went sledding. Moreover, in
the locket in which she treasured a bit of her dead
mother's hair, there was a black pearl as big as a
pea. These things made it difficult—perhaps impossible—for Ralph Hagadorn to say more than, "I
love you." But that much he meant to say though
he were **scourged** with **chagrin** for his **temerity.**

This **determination** grew upon him as he swept
along the ice under the starlight. Venus made a
glowing path toward the west and seemed eager
to reassure him. He was sorry he could not skim
down that avenue of light which flowed from the
love-star, but he was forced to turn his back upon
it and face the black northeast.

illusion *(noun)* an image that is not necessarily true

flutter[ing] *(verb)* to flap

trumpet[ed] *(verb)* to yell in a way that one sounds like a trumpet

tension *(noun)* stress

gleam *(noun)* a partially hidden light

perceive[d] *(verb)* to become aware

hesitate[d] *(verb)* to pause

irresistibly *(adverb)* in a way that makes it impossible to resist

came to him *(idiom)* realized

pursuit *(noun)* a chase

latitude[s] *(noun)* the angular distance from the earth's equator, measured north or south

It came to him with a shock that he was not alone. His eyelashes were frosted and his eyeballs blurred with the cold, so at first he thought it might be an **illusion.** But when he had rubbed his eyes hard, he made sure that not very far in front of him was a long white skater in **fluttering** garments who sped over the ice as fast as ever werewolf went.

He called aloud, but there was no answer. He shaped his hands and **trumpeted** through them, but the silence was as before—it was complete. So then he gave chase, setting his teeth hard and putting a **tension** on his firm young muscles. But go however he would, the white skater went faster. After a time, as he glanced at the cold **gleam** of the north star, he **perceived** that he was being led from his direct path. For a moment he **hesitated,** wondering if he would not better keep to his road, but his weird companion seemed to draw him on **irresistibly,** and finding it sweet to follow, he followed.

Of course it **came to him** more than once in that strange **pursuit,** that the white skater was no earthly guide. Up in those **latitudes** men see curi-

bitter *(adjective)* severe

arrogantly *(adverb)* in an exaggerated, over-
   important manner

beheld *(verb)* to see

glance *(noun)* quick movement of the eyes
momentum *(noun)* strength and speed created
   by motion

ous things when the hoary frost is on the earth. Hagadorn's own father—to hark no further than that for an instance!—who lived up there with the Lake Superior Indians, and worked in the copper mines, had welcomed a woman at his hut one **bitter** night, who was gone by morning, leaving wolf tracks on the snow! Yes, it was so, and John Fontanelle, the half-breed, could tell you about it any day—if he were alive. (Alack, the snow where the wolf tracks were, is melted now!)

Well, Hagadorn followed the white skater all the night, and when the ice flushed pink at dawn, and arrows of lovely light shot up into the cold heavens, she was gone, and Hagadorn was at his destination. The sun climbed **arrogantly** up to his place above all other things, and as Hagadorn took off his skates and glanced carelessly lakeward, he **beheld** a great wind-rift in the ice, and the waves showing blue and hungry between white fields. Had he rushed along his intended path, watching the stars to guide him, his **glance** turned upward, all his body at magnificent **momentum,** he must certainly have gone into that cold grave.

How wonderful that it had been sweet to follow

furor *(noun)* busy activity

starved *(adjective)* lacking food or other necessities

chilled *(adjective)* cold

wandering in her mind *(idiom)* unable to make sense; incoherent

the white skater, and that he followed!

His heart beat hard as he hurried to his friend's house. But he encountered no wedding **furor**. His friend met him as men meet in houses of mourning.

"Is this your wedding face?" cried Hagadorn. "Why, man, **starved** as I am, I look more like a bridegroom than you!"

"There's no wedding to-day!"

"No wedding! Why, you're not—"

"Marie Beaujeu died last night—"

"Marie—"

"Died last night. She had been skating in the afternoon, and she came home **chilled** and **wandering in her mind,** as if the frost had got in it somehow. She grew worse and worse, and all the time she talked of you."

"Of me?"

"We wondered what it meant. No one knew you were lovers."

"I didn't know it myself; more's the pity. At least, I didn't know—"

"She said you were on the ice, and that you didn't know about the big breaking-up, and she

broke in with *(idiom)* interrupted
had come to pass *(idiom)* had happened

intend[ed] *(verb)* to plan

cried to us that the wind was off shore and the rift widening. She cried over and over again that you could come in by the old French creek if you only knew—"

"I came in that way."

"But how did you come to do that? It's out of the path. We thought perhaps—"

But Hagadorn **broke in with** his story and told him all as it **had come to pass.**

That day they watched beside the maiden, who lay with candles at her head and at her feet, and in the little church the bride who might have been at her wedding said prayers for her friend. They buried Marie Beaujeu in her bridesmaid white, and Hagadorn was before the altar with her, as he had **intended** from the first! Then at midnight the lovers who were to wed whispered their vows in the gloom of the cold church, and walked together through the snow to lay their bridal wreaths upon a grave.

Three nights later, Hagadorn skated back again to his home. They wanted him to go by sunlight, but he had his way, and went when Venus made her bright path on the ice.

companion *(noun)* someone who keeps someone else company

bay[ing] *(verb)* the crying of a wolf or wild
animal

defile[d] *(verb)* to contaminate; to make dirty

The truth was, he had hoped for the companion-ship of the white skater. But he did not have it. His only **companion** was the wind. The only voice he heard was the **baying** of a wolf on the north shore. The world was as empty and as white as if God had just created it, and the sun had not yet colored nor man **defiled** it.

accustomed *(adjective)* used to; in the habit of
rough *(adjective)* wild; disturbing
irascible *(adjective)* easily angered or upset

dropped in *(idiom)* stopped by

disorderly *(adverb)* in a confused or unorganized manner
litter *(noun)* a collection of discarded items

A Child of the Rain

by Elia Wilkinson Peattie

It was the night that Mona Meeks, the dressmaker, told him she didn't love him. He couldn't believe it at first, because he had so long been **accustomed** to the idea that she did, and no matter how **rough** the weather or how **irascible** the passengers, he felt a song in his heart as he punched transfers, and rang his bell punch, and signalled the driver when to let people off and on.

Now, suddenly, with no reason except a woman's, she had changed her mind. He **dropped in** to see her at five o'clock, just before time for the night shift, and to give her two red apples he had been saving for her. She looked at the apples as if they were invisible and she could not see them, and standing in her **disorderly** little dressmaking parlor, with its cuttings and scraps and **litter** of fabrics, she said:

"It is no use, John. I shall have to work here like

gasp *(noun)* a loud intake of air as a result of a shock

lumbering *(adjective)* clumsy
strode [stride] *(verb)* to move; to walk

splutter[ing] *(verb)* to make a noise like spitting
gruff *(adjective)* rough; harsh
relieve[d] *(verb)* to take the place of at a task

equilibrium *(noun)* a state of physical balance

judging by the fact *(idiom)* reaching a conclusion based on information

this all my life—work here alone. For I don't love you, John. No, I don't. I thought I did, but it is a mistake."

"You mean it?" asked John, bringing up the words in a great **gasp.**

"Yes," she said, white and trembling and putting out her hands as if to beg for his mercy. And then—big, **lumbering** fool—he turned around and **strode** down the stairs and stood at the corner in the beating rain waiting for his car. It came along at length, **spluttering** on the wet rails and spitting out blue fire, and he took his shift after a **gruff** "Good night" to Johnson, the man he **relieved.**

He was glad the rain was bitter cold and drove in his face fiercely. He rejoiced at the cruelty of the wind, and when it hustled pedestrians before it, lashing them, twisting their clothes, and threatening their **equilibrium,** he felt amused. He was pleased at the chill in his bones and at the hunger that tortured him. At least, at first he thought it was hunger till he remembered that he had just eaten. The hours passed confusedly. He had no consciousness of time. But it must have been late,—near midnight,—**judging by the fact**

curious *(adjective)* unexpected; strange

frayed *(adjective)* worn away
unkempt *(adjective)* untidy; not combed or
    brushed
bent *(adjective)* not straight; not even

wrought *(adjective)* made; decorated
stout *(adjective)* strong; study

suggestive of *(idiom)* implied or suggested
fatigue *(noun)* extreme tiredness

that there were few persons visible anywhere in the black storm, when he noticed a little figure sitting at the far end of the car. He had not seen the child when she got on, but all was so **curious** and wild to him that evening—he himself seemed to himself the most curious and the wildest of all things—that it was not surprising that he should not have observed the little creature.

She was wrapped in a coat so much too large that it had become **frayed** at the bottom from dragging on the pavement. Her hair hung in **unkempt** stringiness about her **bent** shoulders, and her feet were covered with old boots, many sizes too big, from which the soles hung loose.

Beside the little figure was a chest of dark wood, with curiously **wrought** hasps. From this depended a **stout** strap by which it could be carried over the shoulders. John Billings stared in, fascinated by the poor little thing with its head sadly drooping upon its breast, its thin blue hands relaxed upon its lap, and its whole attitude so **suggestive of** hunger, loneliness, and **fatigue,** that he made up his mind he would collect no fare from it.

plunge[d] *(verb)* to move along quickly and
   roughly

owing to *(idiom)* because of; as a result of
obscured *(adjective)* hidden

grow [anxious] *(idiom)* to become more and
   more

intend[ing] *(verb)* to plan

flickering *(noun)* irregular movement of light
halting *(noun)* a sudden stopping
reassert[ed] *(verb)* to show once again that
   something exists

"It will need its nickel for breakfast," he said to himself. "The company can stand this for once. Or, come to think of it, I might celebrate my hard luck. Here's to the brotherhood of failures!" And he took a nickel from one pocket of his great-coat and dropped it in another, ringing his bell punch to record the transfer.

The car **plunged** along in the darkness, and the rain beat more viciously than ever in his face. The night was full of the rushing sound of the storm. **Owing to** some change of temperature the glass of the car became **obscured** so that the young conductor could no longer see the little figure distinctly, and he **grew** anxious about the child.

"I wonder if it's all right," he said to himself. "I never saw a living creature sit so still."

He opened the car door, **intending** to speak with the child, but just then something went wrong with the lights. There was a blue and green **flickering,** then darkness, a sudden **halting** of the car, and a great sweep of wind and rain in at the door. When, after a moment, light and motion **reasserted** themselves, and Billings had got the door together, he turned to look at the little pas-

address[ing] *(verb)* to speak directly to
cloak *(noun)* an article of clothing like a jacket
crossly *(adverb)* in an angry or frustrated
    manner
draught *(noun)* wind entering an indoor space

hind *(adjective)* back; rear

ruffle[d] *(verb)* to move through

crouching *(adjective)* lying close to the ground

senger. But the car was empty.

It was a fact. There was no child there—not even moisture on the seat where she had been sitting.

"Bill," said he, going to the front door and **addressing** the driver, "what became of that little kid in the old **cloak**?"

"I didn't see no kid," said Bill, **crossly.** "For Gawd's sake, close the door, John, and git that **draught** off my back."

"Draught!" said John, indignantly, "where's the draught?" "You've left the **hind** door open," growled Bill, and John saw him shivering as a blast struck him and **ruffled** the fur on his bear-skin coat. But the door was not open, and yet John had to admit to himself that the car seemed filled with wind and a strange coldness.

However, it didn't matter. Nothing mattered! Still, it was as well no doubt to look under the seats just to make sure no little **crouching** figure was there, and so he did. But there was nothing. In fact, John said to himself, he seemed to be getting expert in finding nothing where there ought to be something.

He might have stayed in the car, for there was

likelihood *(noun)* probability; possibility

drench *(verb)* to soak through with water
pommel *(verb)* to beat
blare *(noun)* harsh sight or colors

lurch *(noun)* a quick jump or roll

instinctively *(adverb)* in a spontaneous or natural manner; done without thinking
pant[ing] *(verb)* to breathe heavily
doze[d] *(verb)* to fall into a light sleep

half-stifled *(adjective)* partially held back

eerie *(adjective)* strange; odd

no **likelihood** of more passengers that evening, but somehow he preferred going out where the rain could **drench** him and the wind **pommel** him. How horribly tired he was! If there were only some still place away from the **blare** of the city where a man could lie down and listen to the sound of the sea or the storm—or if one could grow suddenly old and get through with the bother of living—or if—

The car gave a sudden **lurch** as it rounded a curve, and for a moment it seemed to be a mere chance whether Conductor Billings would stay on his platform or go off under those fire-spitting wheels. He caught **instinctively** at his brake, saved himself, and stood still for a moment, **panting.**

"I must have **dozed,**" he said to himself.

Just then, dimly, through the blurred window, he saw again the little figure of the child, its head on its breast as before, its blue hands lying in its lap and the curious box beside it. John Billings felt a coldness beyond the coldness of the night run through his blood. Then, with a **half-stifled** cry, he threw back the door, and made a desperate spring at the corner where the **eerie** thing sat.

wretch *(noun)* an unfortunate person

roar[ed] *(verb)* to speak loudly

mutter[ed] *(verb)* to say something without
speaking clearly or loudly

sank to sleep *(idiom)* fall asleep; go to sleep
hearty *(adjective)* strong; healthy

And he touched the green carpeting on the seat, which was quite dry and warm, as if no dripping, miserable little **wretch** had ever crouched there.

He rushed to the front door.

"Bill," he **roared,** "I want to know about that kid."

"What kid?"

"The same kid! The wet one with the old coat and the box with iron hasps! The one that's been sitting here in the car!"

Bill turned his surly face to confront the young conductor.

"You've been drinking, you fool," said he. "Fust thing you know you'll be reported."

The conductor said not a word. He went slowly and weakly back to his post and stood there the rest of the way leaning against the end of the car for support. Once or twice he **muttered:**

"The poor little brat!" And again he said, "So you didn't love me after all!"

He never knew how he reached home, but he **sank to sleep** as dying men sink to death. All the same, being a **hearty** young man, he was on duty again next day but one, and again the night was

47

shock *(noun)* impact

summon[ed] *(verb)* to call into action

weather-beaten *(adjective)* damaged by the
weather

rainy and cold.

It was the last run, and the car was spinning along at its limit, when there came a sudden soft **shock**. John Billings knew what that meant. He had felt something of the kind once before. He turned sick for a moment, and held on to the brake. Then he **summoned** his courage and went around to the side of the car, which had stopped. Bill, the driver, was before him, and had a limp little figure in his arms, and was carrying it to the gaslight. John gave one look and cried:

"It's the same kid, Bill! The one I told you of!"

True as truth were the ragged coat dangling from the pitiful body, the little blue hands, the thin shoulders, the stringy hair, the big boots on the feet. And in the road not far off was the curious chest of dark wood with iron hasps.

"She ran under the car deliberate!" cried Bill. "I yelled to her, but she looked at me and ran straight on!"

He was white in spite of his **weather-beaten** skin.

"I guess you wasn't drunk last night after all, John," said he.

"You—you are sure the kid is—is there?" gasped John.

"Not so damned sure!" said Bill.

But a few minutes later it was taken away in a patrol wagon, and with it the little box with iron hasps.

berth *(noun)* a seat

lucidity *(noun)* clear in thought

hurry[ing] *(verb)* to go quickly

aisle *(noun)* a passageway between rows of seats
restlessly *(adverb)* in an uneasy way
irritated/irritability *(adjective/noun)* annoyed/
    the state of being annoyed
petulance *(noun)* the state of being rude or
    badly behaved
imperceptible *(adjective)* not able to be sensed
estrangement *(noun)* the state of being removed
    from a relationship; alienation

A Journey

by Edith Wharton

As she lay in her **berth,** staring at the shadows overhead, the rush of the wheels was in her brain, driving her deeper and deeper into circles of wakeful **lucidity.** The sleeping-car had sunk into its night-silence. Through the wet window-pane she watched the sudden lights, the long stretches of **hurrying** blackness. Now and then she turned her head and looked through the opening in the hangings at her husband's curtains across the **aisle**....

She wondered **restlessly** if he wanted anything and if she could hear him if he called. His voice had grown very weak within the last months and it **irritated** him when she did not hear. This irritability, this increasing childish **petulance** seemed to give expression to their **imperceptible estrangement.** Like two faces looking at one another through a sheet of glass they were close

conductivity *(noun)* the ability to transmit something

impenetrably *(adverb)* in a manner that is unable to be accessed

irrelevancies *(noun)* something not relevant; something not applicable to anything else

tinged *(adjective)* colored; modified

prodigal *(adjective)* very extravagant or wasteful

preempt[ing] *(verb)* to stall; to keep from happening

arrears *(noun)* an unfinished task

reluctant *(adjective)* hesitant; unwilling

together, almost touching, but they could not hear or feel each other: the **conductivity** between them was broken. She, at least, had this sense of separation, and she fancied sometimes that she saw it reflected in the look with which he supplemented his failing words. Doubtless the fault was hers. She was too **impenetrably** healthy to be touched by the **irrelevancies** of disease. Her self-reproachful tenderness was **tinged** with the sense of his irrationality: she had a vague feeling that there was a purpose in his helpless tyrannies. The suddenness of the change had found her so unprepared. A year ago their pulses had beat to one robust measure; both had the same **prodigal** confidence in an exhaustless future. Now their energies no longer kept step: hers still bounded ahead of life, **preempting** unclaimed regions of hope and activity, while his lagged behind, vainly struggling to overtake her.

When they married, she had such **arrears** of living to make up: her days had been as bare as the whitewashed school-room where she forced innutritious facts upon **reluctant** children. His coming had broken in on the slumber of circumstance,

encloser *(noun)* outer boundary; limit

remote *(adjective)* far off; unachievable

from the first *(idiom)* right away; immediately

beset *(verb)* to be troubled by

evasive *(adjective)* intentionally vague or
ambiguous

temperament *(noun)* a common or typical
response

undefinably *(adverb)* in a manner that cannot
be explained or defined

importunities *(noun)* troubles; difficulties

widening the present till it became the **encloser** of **remotest** chances. But imperceptibly the horizon narrowed. Life had a grudge against her: she was never to be allowed to spread her wings.

At first the doctors had said that six weeks of mild air would set him right; but when he came back this assurance was explained as having of course included a winter in a dry climate. They gave up their pretty house, storing the wedding presents and new furniture, and went to Colorado. She had hated it there **from the first.** Nobody knew her or cared about her; there was no one to wonder at the good match she had made, or to envy her the new dresses and the visiting-cards which were still a surprise to her. And he kept growing worse. She felt herself **beset** with difficulties too **evasive** to be fought by so direct a **temperament.** She still loved him, of course; but he was gradually, **undefinably** ceasing to be himself. The man she had married had been strong, active, gently masterful: the male whose pleasure it is to clear a way through the material obstructions of life; but now it was she who was the protector, he who must be shielded from **importunities** and given

bewilder[ed] *(verb)* to confuse

punctual *(adjective)* on time

administering [of medicine] *(idiom)* to give [something]

gushes *(noun)* an outpouring

instinctive *(adjective)* without thinking; spontaneous

resentment *(noun)* feeling against someone or something

grope[d] *(verb)* to feel without being certain

hoarse *(adjective)* having a harsh or rough sound

furtively *(adverb)* in a secretive manner

leniently *(adverb)* in an easy and tolerant manner

his drops or his beef-juice though the skies were falling. The routine of the sick-room **bewildered** her; this **punctual administering** of medicine seemed as idle as some uncomprehended religious mummery.

There were moments, indeed, when warm **gushes** of pity swept away her **instinctive resentment** of his condition, when she still found his old self in his eyes as they **groped** for each other through the dense medium of his weakness. But these moments had grown rare. Sometimes he frightened her: his sunken expressionless face seemed that of a stranger; his voice was weak and **hoarse;** his thin-lipped smile a mere muscular contraction. Her hand avoided his damp soft skin, which had lost the familiar roughness of health: she caught herself **furtively** watching him as she might have watched a strange animal. It frightened her to feel that this was the man she loved; there were hours when to tell him what she suffered seemed the one escape from her fears. But in general she judged herself more **leniently,** reflecting that she had perhaps been too long alone with him, and that she would feel differently when they were at home

buoyant *(adjective)* happy; cheerful

consent *(noun)* permission; approval

euphuisms *(noun)* elegant but false statements

allusion *(noun)* reference; hint

treacheries *(noun)* betrayal; trick
in reserve *(idiom)* stockpiled; left over

chafe *(verb)* to rub; to irritate
dispassionate *(adjective)* without strong feeling
or emotion

again, surrounded by her robust and **buoyant** family. How she had rejoiced when the doctors at last gave their **consent** to his going home! She knew, of course, what the decision meant; they both knew. It meant that he was to die; but they dressed the truth in hopeful **euphuisms,** and at times, in the joy of preparation, she really forgot the purpose of their journey, and slipped into an eager **allusion** to next year's plans.

At last the day of leaving came. She had a dreadful fear that they would never get away; that somehow at the last moment he would fail her; that the doctors held one of their accustomed **treacheries in reserve;** but nothing happened. They drove to the station, he was installed in a seat with a rug over his knees and a cushion at his back, and she hung out of the window waving unregretful farewells to the acquaintances she had really never liked till then.

The first twenty-four hours had passed off well. He revived a little and it amused him to look out of the window and to observe the humours of the car. The second day he began to grow weary and to **chafe** under the **dispassionate** stare of the freck-

sentiment *(noun)* feeling; emotion

punctuated *(adjective)* interrupted occasionally
irritations *(noun)* annoyances

hover[ed] *(verb)* to move back and forth

imperturbably *(adverb)* in a calm or relaxed
  manner
linger[ed] *(verb)* to move in a slow way
proffers *(noun)* offer
philanthropic *(adjective)* dedicated to helping
  others
audibly *(adverb)* in a way that can be heard

led child with the lump of chewing-gum. She had to explain to the child's mother that her husband was too ill to be disturbed: a statement received by that lady with a resentment visibly supported by the maternal **sentiment** of the whole car....

That night he slept badly and the next morning his temperature frightened her: she was sure he was growing worse. The day passed slowly, **punctuated** by the small **irritations** of travel. Watching his tired face, she traced in its contractions every rattle and jolt of the tram, till her own body vibrated with sympathetic fatigue. She felt the others observing him too, and **hovered** restlessly between him and the line of interrogative eyes. The freckled child hung about him like a fly; offers of candy and picture-books failed to dislodge her: she twisted one leg around the other and watched him **imperturbably.** The porter, as he passed, **lingered** with vague **proffers** of help, probably inspired by **philanthropic** passengers swelling with the sense that "something ought to be done;" and one nervous man in a skull-cap was **audibly** concerned as to the possible effect on his wife's health.

dreary *(adjective)* discouraging; gloomy

inoccupation *(noun)* the state of doing nothing or not being busy

pang *(noun)* a sudden but brief pain

people *(noun)* relatives

pressing through *(idiom)* pushing through; moving through

splendidly *(adverb)* in a grand or superb manner

subtler *(adjective)* refined; insightful

coarseness *(noun)* roughness; harshness

The hours dragged on in a **dreary inoccupation.** Towards dusk she sat down beside him and he laid his hand on hers. The touch startled her. He seemed to be calling her from far off. She looked at him helplessly and his smile went through her like a physical **pang.**

"Are you very tired?" she asked.

"No, not very."

"We'll be there soon now."

"Yes, very soon."

"This time to-morrow—"

He nodded and they sat silent. When she had put him to bed and crawled into her own berth she tried to cheer herself with the thought that in less than twenty-four hours they would be in New York. Her **people** would all be at the station to meet her—she pictured their round unanxious faces **pressing through** the crowd. She only hoped they would not tell him too loudly that he was looking **splendidly** and would be all right in no time: the **subtler** sympathies developed by long contact with suffering were making her aware of a certain **coarseness** of texture in the family sensibilities.

greasy *(adjective)* oily

tendency *(noun)* habit; trend
fasten *(verb)* to attach; to secure
intolerable *(adjective)* unbearable; extreme
foreboding[s] *(noun)* a worry about or prediction of something bad happening
impulse *(noun)* an instant need to do something

restrain[ed] *(verb)* to stop; to prevent
reassure[d] *(verb)* to give a feeling of confidence

endure *(verb)* to continue; to support

Suddenly she thought she heard him call. She parted the curtains and listened. No, it was only a man snoring at the other end of the car. His snores had a **greasy** sound, as though they passed through tallow. She lay down and tried to sleep... Had she not heard him move? She started up trembling... The silence frightened her more than any sound. He might not be able to make her hear—he might be calling her now... What made her think of such things? It was merely the familiar **tendency** of an over-tired mind to **fasten** itself on the most **intolerable** chance within the range of its **forebodings**.... Putting her head out, she listened; but she could not distinguish his breathing from that of the other pairs of lungs about her. She longed to get up and look at him, but she knew the **impulse** was a mere vent for her restlessness, and the fear of disturbing him **restrained** her.... The regular movement of his curtain **reassured** her, she knew not why; she remembered that he had wished her a cheerful good-night; and the sheer inability to **endure** her fears a moment longer made her put them from her with an effort of her whole sound tired body. She turned on her side and slept.

stiffly *(adverb)* in a rigid manner

keen *(adjective)* intense

stir[ring] *(verb)* to begin to move

dishevelled *(adjective)* marked by disorder

struggle *(noun)* challenge; effort

deliciously *(adverb)* in a sensually appealing manner

broke into *(idiom)* to begin to

elasticity *(noun)* the ability to recover to original form; resilience

She sat up **stiffly,** staring out at the dawn. The train was rushing through a region of bare hills huddled against a lifeless sky. It looked like the first day of creation. The air of the car was close, and she pushed up her window to let in **the keen** wind. Then she looked at her watch: it was seven o'clock, and soon the people about her would be **stirring.** She slipped into her clothes, smoothed her **dishevelled** hair and crept to the dressing-room. When she had washed her face and adjusted her dress she felt more hopeful. It was always a **struggle** for her not to be cheerful in the morning. Her cheeks burned **deliciously** under the coarse towel and the wet hair about her temples **broke into** strong upward tendrils. Every inch of her was full of life and **elasticity.** And in ten hours they would be at home!

She stepped to her husband's berth: it was time for him to take his early glass of milk. The window-shade was down, and in the dusk of the curtained enclosure she could just see that he lay sideways, with his face away from her. She leaned over him and drew up the shade. As she did so she touched one of his hands. It felt cold....

shrinkingly *(adverb)* in a manner that shows recoil or repulsion

sickening *(adjective)* revolting

steady *(adjective)* not moving; fixed

longing to *(idiom)* wanting to; desiring to

fly from him *(idiom)* get away from as fast as possible

arrest[ed] *(verb)* to stop; to halt

thrust *(verb)* to push; to shove

She bent closer, laying her hand on his arm and calling him by name. He did not move. She spoke again more loudly; she grasped his shoulder and gently shook it. He lay motionless. She caught hold of his hand again: it slipped from her limply, like a dead thing. A dead thing? ... Her breath caught. She must see his face. She leaned forward, and hurriedly, **shrinkingly,** with a **sickening** reluctance of the flesh, laid her hands on his shoulders and turned him over. His head fell back; his face looked small and smooth; he gazed at her with **steady** eyes.

She remained motionless for a long time, holding him thus; and they looked at each other. Suddenly she shrank back: the **longing to** scream, to call out, to **fly from him,** had almost overpowered her. But a strong hand **arrested** her. Good God! If it were known that he was dead they would be put off the train at the next station—

In a terrifying flash of remembrance there arose before her a scene she had once witnessed in travelling, when a husband and wife, whose child had died in the train, had been **thrust** out at some

chance *(adjective)* random

dazed *(adjective)* stunned
receding *(adjective)* withdrawing; retreating

cower[ed] *(verb)* to crouch; to shrink

gesture *(noun)* movement

outstretched *(adjective)* extended; stretched out

sepulchral *(adjective)* funeral-like
conceal *(verb)* to hide

clutch[ing] *(verb)* to hold; to grasp

chance station. She saw them standing on the platform with the child's body between them; she had never forgotten the **dazed** look with which they followed the **receding** train. And this was what would happen to her. Within the next hour she might find herself on the platform of some strange station, alone with her husband's body.... Anything but that! It was too horrible—She quivered like a creature at bay.

As she **cowered** there, she felt the train moving more slowly. It was coming then—they were approaching a station! She saw again the husband and wife standing on the lonely platform; and with a violent **gesture** she drew down the shade to hide her husband's face.

Feeling dizzy, she sank down on the edge of the berth, keeping away from his **outstretched** body, and pulling the curtains close, so that he and she were shut into a kind of **sepulchral** twilight. She tried to think. At all costs she must **conceal** the fact that he was dead. But how? Her mind refused to act: she could not plan, combine. She could think of no way but to sit there, **clutching** the curtains, all day long....

rouse *(verb)* to wake up; to excite
supreme *(adjective)* highest

part[ed] *(verb)* to separate

burden *(noun)* heavy load
glance[d] *(verb)* to look at quickly

She heard the porter making up her bed; people were beginning to move about the car; the dressing-room door was being opened and shut. She tried to **rouse** herself. At length with a **supreme** effort she rose to her feet, stepping into the aisle of the car and drawing the curtains tight behind her. She noticed that they still **parted** slightly with the motion of the car, and finding a pin in her dress she fastened them together. Now she was safe. She looked round and saw the porter. She fancied he was watching her.

"Ain't he awake yet?" he enquired.

"No," she faltered.

"I got his milk all ready when he wants it. You know you told me to have it for him by seven."

She nodded silently and crept into her seat.

At half-past eight the train reached Buffalo. By this time the other passengers were dressed and the berths had been folded back for the day. The porter, moving to and fro under his **burden** of sheets and pillows, **glanced** at her as he passed. At length he said: "Ain't he going to get up? You know we're ordered to make up the berths as early as we can."

stammer[ed] *(verb)* to speak in a halting manner

whirling *(adjective)* spinning

expectantly *(adverb)* in a manner that shows anticipation or waiting

semi-obscurity *(noun)* the state of being partially hidden

drew down [the lids] *(idiom)* pulled down

She turned cold with fear. They were just entering the station.

"Oh, not yet," she **stammered.** "Not till he's had his milk. Won't you get it, please?"

"All right. Soon as we start again."

When the train moved on he reappeared with the milk. She took it from him and sat vaguely looking at it: her brain moved slowly from one idea to another, as though they were stepping-stones set far apart across a **whirling** flood. At length she became aware that the porter still hovered **expectantly.**

"Will I give it to him?" he suggested.

"Oh, no," she cried, rising. "He—he's asleep yet, I think—" She waited till the porter had passed on; then she unpinned the curtains and slipped behind them. In the **semi-obscurity** her husband's face stared up at her like a marble mask with agate eyes. The eyes were dreadful. She put out her hand and **drew down** the lids. Then she remembered the glass of milk in her other hand: what was she to do with it? She thought of raising the window and throwing it out; but to do so she would have to lean across his body and bring her face close to

77

party *(noun)* a person or group of people

intimate *(adjective)* familiar; offering warmth

remarkable *(adjective)* noticeable; extraordinary

rebuff *(noun)* rejection; snub
indulgently *(adverb)* in a tolerant manner

his. She decided to drink the milk.

She returned to her seat with the empty glass and after a while the porter came back to get it.

"When'll I fold up his bed?" he asked.

"Oh, not now—not yet; he's ill—he's very ill. Can't you let him stay as he is? The doctor wants him to lie down as much as possible."

He scratched his head. "Well, if he's—really—sick—"

He took the empty glass and walked away, explaining to the passengers that the **party** behind the curtains was too sick to get up just yet.

She found herself the center of sympathetic eyes. A motherly woman with an **intimate** smile sat down beside her.

"I'm real sorry to hear your husband's sick. I've had a **remarkable** amount of sickness in my family and maybe I could assist you. Can I take a look at him?"

"Oh, no—no, please! He mustn't be disturbed."

The lady accepted the **rebuff indulgently.**

"Well, it's just as you say, of course, but you don't look to me as if you'd had much experience in sickness and I'd have been glad to assist you.

oftener *(adverb)* more frequently

press upon *(idiom)* crowd in on

prominent *(adjective)* noticeable
projecting *(adjective)* forward

waylaid *(verb)* to hide and wait for an attack

What do you generally do when your husband's taken this way?"

"I—I let him sleep."

"Too much sleep ain't any too healthful either. Don't you give him any medicine?"

"Y—yes."

"Don't you wake him to take it?"

"Yes."

"When does he take the next dose?"

"Not for—two hours—"

The lady looked disappointed. "Well, if I was you I'd try giving it **oftener.** That's what I do with my folks."

After that many faces seemed to **press upon** her. The passengers were on their way to the dining-car, and she was conscious that as they passed down the aisle they glanced curiously at the closed curtains. One lantern-jawed man with **prominent** eyes stood still and tried to shoot his **projecting** glance through the division between the folds. The freckled child, returning from breakfast, **way-laid** the passers with a buttery clutch, saying in a loud whisper, "He's sick;" and once the conductor came by, asking for tickets. She shrank into her

fantastically *(adverb)* in an unbelievable or
    unreal manner

creased *(adjective)* wrinkled

apostolic *(adjective)* apostle-like

delusion *(noun)* a false belief
influx *(noun)* an invasion or coming in of
    something
passively *(adverb)* in a non-aggressive manner
dissolution *(noun)* death; decay
cease *(verb)* to stop entirely

corner and looked out of the window at the flying trees and houses, meaningless hieroglyphs of an endlessly unrolled papyrus.

Now and then the train stopped, and the new-comers on entering the car stared in turn at the closed curtains. More and more people seemed to pass—their faces began to blend **fantastically** with the images surging in her brain....

Later in the day a fat man detached himself from the mist of faces. He had a **creased** stomach and soft pale lips. As he pressed himself into the seat facing her she noticed that he was dressed in black broadcloth, with a soiled white tie.

"Husband's pretty bad this morning, is he?"

"Yes."

"Dear, dear! Now that's terribly distressing, ain't it?" An **apostolic** smile revealed his gold-filled teeth.

"Of course you know there's no such thing as sickness. Ain't that a lovely thought? Death itself is but a **delusion** of our grosser senses. Only lay yourself open to the **influx** of the sprirt, submit yourself **passively** to the action of the divine force, and disease and **dissolution** will **cease** to exist for

induce *(verb)* to persuade; to cause to do
    something

indistinct *(adjective)* unclear; unrecognizable

recollection *(noun)* memory

ardently *(adverb)* in an eager manner

relative *(adjective)* dependent; comparative

maintain[ing] *(verb)* to affirm; to assert

effect[ed] *(verb)* to cause to happen

precipice *(noun)* a steep location

vividly *(adverb)* in a clear manner

you. If you could **induce** your husband to read this little pamphlet—"

The faces about her again grew **indistinct**. She had a vague **recollection** of hearing the motherly lady and the parent of the freckled child **ardently** disputing the **relative** advantages of trying several medicines at once, or of taking each in turn; the motherly lady **maintaining** that the competitive system saved time; the other objecting that you couldn't tell which remedy had **effected** the cure; their voices went on and on, like bell-buoys droning through a fog.... The porter came up now and then with questions that she did not understand, but that somehow she must have answered since he went away again without repeating them; every two hours the motherly lady reminded her that her husband ought to have his drops; people left the car and others replaced them...

Her head was spinning and she tried to steady herself by clutching at her thoughts as they swept by, but they slipped away from her like bushes on the side of a sheer **precipice** down which she seemed to be falling. Suddenly her mind grew clear again and she found herself **vividly** picturing

gradually *(adverb)* in a slowly proceeding
  manner
clamorously *(adverb)* in a busy or noisy manner

unguarded *(adjective)* careless; unprotected

murmur[ing] *(verb)* to speak in a quiet and
  unclear manner

what would happen when the train reached New York. She shuddered as it occurred to her that he would be quite cold and that some one might perceive he had been dead since morning.

She thought hurriedly:—"If they see I am not surprised they will suspect something. They will ask questions, and if I tell them the truth they won't believe me—no one would believe me! It will be terrible"—and she kept repeating to herself:—"I must pretend I don't know. I must pretend I don't know. When they open the curtains I must go up to him quite naturally—and then I must scream." ... She had an idea that the scream would be very hard to do.

Gradually new thoughts crowded upon her, vivid and urgent: she tried to separate and restrain them, but they beset her **clamorously,** like her school-children at the end of a hot day, when she was too tired to silence them. Her head grew confused, and she felt a sick fear of forgetting her part, of betraying herself by some **unguarded** word or look.

"I must pretend I don't know," she went on **murmuring**. The words had lost their significance,

monotonous *(adjective)* unchanging; uniform

intricate *(adjective)* complicated; detailed

fixedly *(adverb)* in an unmoving manner

avert *(verb)* to avoid; to turn away

vice *(noun)* an instrument used to hold something together or in place

suspended *(adjective)* hanging; dangling

but she repeated them mechanically, as though they had been a magic formula, until suddenly she heard herself saying: "I can't remember, I can't remember!"

Her voice sounded very loud, and she looked about her in terror; but no one seemed to notice that she had spoken.

As she glanced down the car her eye caught the curtains of her husband's berth, and she began to examine the **monotonous** arabesques woven through their heavy folds. The pattern was **intricate** and difficult to trace; she gazed **fixedly** at the curtains and as she did so the thick stuff grew transparent and through it she saw her husband's face—his dead face. She struggled to **avert** her look, but her eyes refused to move and her head seemed to be held in a **vice.** At last, with an effort that left her weak and shaking, she turned away; but it was of no use; close in front of her, small and smooth, was her husband's face. It seemed to be **suspended** in the air between her and the false braids of the woman who sat in front of her.

With an uncontrollable gesture she stretched out her hand to push the face away, and suddenly she

repress[ed] *(verb)* to hold in; to subdue

justify *(verb)* to make known that something is
    right or reasonable

haste *(noun)* quickness; speed

waxen *(adjective)* looking like wax; pale

elapse[d] *(verb)* to pass

dread[ed] *(verb)* to fear

hastily *(adverb)* in a quick or hurried manner

felt the touch of his smooth skin. She **repressed** a cry and half started from her seat. The woman with the false braids looked around, and feeling that she must **justify** her movement in some way she rose and lifted her travelling-bag from the opposite seat. She unlocked the bag and looked into it; but the first object her hand met was a small flask of her husband's, thrust there at the last moment, in the **haste** of departure. She locked the bag and closed her eyes ... his face was there again, hanging between her eye-balls and lids like a **waxen** mask against a red curtain....

She roused herself with a shiver. Had she fainted or slept? Hours seemed to have **elapsed**; but it was still broad day, and the people about her were sitting in the same attitudes as before.

A sudden sense of hunger made her aware that she had eaten nothing since morning. The thought of food filled her with disgust, but she **dreaded** a return of faintness, and remembering that she had some biscuits in her bag she took one out and ate it. The dry crumbs choked her, and she **hastily** swallowed a little brandy from her husband's flask. The burning sensation in her throat acted as a

counter-irritant *(noun)* something that acts against an annoyance

momentarily *(adverb)* for a brief amount of time

quietude *(noun)* restfulness

impetuous *(adjective)* known for being quick to act or passionate

inexorable *(adjective)* unstoppable; relentless

pulsation *(noun)* heartbeat; throb

prolonged *(adjective)* extended; continuous

counter-irritant, momentarily relieving the dull ache of her nerves. Then she felt a gently-stealing warmth, as though a soft air fanned her, and the swarming fears relaxed their clutch, receding through the stillness that enclosed her, a stillness soothing as the spacious **quietude** of a summer day. She slept.

Through her sleep she felt the **impetuous** rush of the train. It seemed to be life itself that was sweeping her on with headlong **inexorable** force— sweeping her into darkness and terror, and the awe of unknown days.—Now all at once everything was still—not a sound, not a **pulsation**... She was dead in her turn, and lay beside him with smooth upstaring face. How quiet it was!—and yet she heard feet coming, the feet of the men who were to carry them away... She could feel too—she felt a sudden **prolonged** vibration, a series of hard shocks, and then another plunge into darkness: the darkness of death this time—a black whirlwind on which they were both spinning like leaves, in wild uncoiling spirals, with millions and millions of the dead....

* * * * *

impartial *(adjective)* known for treating everything and everyone equally

impersonal *(adjective)* not having specific qualities; indefinite

expanse *(noun)* a large spreading out space

sooty *(adjective)* covered in soot or ash

dilate[d] *(verb)* to enlarge; to swell

meditatively *(adverb)* in a thoughtful or reflective manner

revolve[ing] *(verb)* to turn; to rotate

She sprang up in terror. Her sleep must have lasted a long time, for the winter day had paled and the lights had been lit. The car was in confusion, and as she regained her self-possession she saw that the passengers were gathering up their wraps and bags. The woman with the false braids had brought from the dressing-room a sickly ivy-plant in a bottle, and the Christian Scientist was reversing his cuffs. The porter passed down the aisle with his **impartial** brush. An **impersonal** figure with a gold-banded cap asked for her husband's ticket. A voice shouted "Baig-gage express!" and she heard the clicking of metal as the passengers handed over their checks.

Presently her window was blocked by an **expanse** of **sooty** wall, and the train passed into the Harlem tunnel. The journey was over; in a few minutes she would see her family pushing their joyous way through the throng at the station. Her heart **dilated**. The worst terror was past....

"We'd better get him up now, hadn't we?" asked the porter, touching her arm.

He had her husband's hat in his hand and was **meditatively revolving** it under his brush.

She looked at the hat and tried to speak; but suddenly the car grew dark. She flung up her arms, struggling to catch at something, and fell face downward, striking her head against the dead man's berth.

dismay *(noun)* disappointment
equivalent *(noun)* equal to

wayside *(adjective)* next to a road
hostelry *(noun)* hotel

extant *(adjective)* in existence; on display
prominently *(adverb)* in a noticeable manner

oust[ed] *(verb)* to remove; to eject
march of progress *(idiom)* the passing of time;
    advancing of society

The Vacant Lot

by Mary Wilkins Freeman

When it became generally known in Townsend Center that the Townsends were going to move to the city, there was great excitement and **dismay**. For the Townsends to move was about **equivalent** to the town's moving. The Townsend ancestors had founded the village a hundred years ago. The first Townsend had kept a **wayside hostelry** for man and beast, known as the "Sign of the Leopard." The sign-board, on which the leopard was painted a bright blue, was still **extant**, and **prominently** so, being nailed over the present Townsend's front door. This Townsend, by name David, kept the village store. There had been no tavern since the railroad was built through Townsend Center in his father's day. Therefore the family, being **ousted** by the **march of progress** from their chosen employment, took up with a general country store as being the next thing to a

principal *(adjective)* main; most important

transients *(noun)* people without permanent homes

stray *(adjective)* leftover; unused

deplenishment *(noun)* a decrease; reduction

matrimonial *(adjective)* relating to marriage

inducement *(noun)* a persuasive argument to do something

surmise[d] *(verb)* to infer; to guess without having much information

suitor *(noun)* one who wants to become the romantic partner of another

country tavern, the **principal** difference consisting in the fact that all the guests were **transients,** never requiring bedchambers, securing their rest on the tops of sugar and flour barrels and codfish boxes, and their refreshment from **stray** nibblings at the stock in trade, to the profitless **deplenishment** of raisins and loaf sugar and crackers and cheese.

The flitting of the Townsends from the home of their ancestors was due to a sudden access of wealth from the death of a relative and the desire of Mrs. Townsend to secure better advantages for her son George, sixteen years old, in the way of education, and for her daughter Adrianna, ten years older, better **matrimonial** opportunities. However, this last **inducement** for leaving Townsend Center was not openly stated, only ingeniously **surmised** by the neighbours.

"Sarah Townsend don't think there's anybody in Townsend Center fit for her Adrianna to marry, and so she's goin' to take her to Boston to see if she can't pick up somebody there," they said. Then they wondered what Abel Lyons would do. He had been a humble **suitor** for Adrianna for years,

repulse[d] *(verb)* to repel

ambitious *(adjective)* having high goals or
  ambitions
pugnaciously *(adverb)* in a combative or argu-
  mentative manner
dispose[d] to *(verb)* to be inclined to; to be
  willing
yield[ed] *(verb)* to give in to; to submit

retrograde[d] *(verb)* to decline; to go back

fiery *(adjective)* emotional; spirited

but her mother had not approved, and Adrianna, who was dutiful, had **repulsed** him delicately and rather sadly. He was the only love interest whom she had ever had, and she felt sorry and grateful; she was a plain, awkward girl, and had a patient recognition of the fact.

But her mother was **ambitious**, more so than her father, who was rather **pugnaciously** satisfied with what he had, and not easily **disposed to** change. However, he **yielded** to his wife and consented to sell out his business and purchase a house in Boston and move there.

David Townsend was curiously unlike the line of ancestors from whom he had come. He had either **retrograded** or advanced, as one might look at it. His moral character was certainly better, but he had not the **fiery** spirit and eager grasp at advantage which had distinguished them. Indeed, the old Townsends, though prominent and respected as men of property and influence, had reputations not above suspicions. There was more than one dark whisper regarding them handed down from mother to son in the village, and especially was this true of the first Townsend,

hideous *(adjective)* repulsive; offensive

roistering *(noun)* noisy partying; carousing

high hand *(idiom)* a way of being controlling or
  dominant
imperious *(adjective)* dominant; domineering
competence *(noun)* sufficient funds

shrewdness *(noun)* cleverness
evince[d] *(verb)* to make evident; to reveal

lair *(noun)* resting place; hiding place

he who built the tavern bearing the Sign of the Blue Leopard. His portrait, a **hideous** effort of contemporary art, hung in the garret of David Townsend's home. There was many a tale of wild **roistering**, if no worse, in that old roadhouse, and high stakes, and quarreling in cups, and blows, and money gotten in evil fashion, and the matter hushed up with a **high hand** for inquirers by the **imperious** Townsends who terrorized everybody. David Townsend terrorized nobody. He had gotten his little **competence** from his store by honest methods—the exchanging of sterling goods and true weights for country produce and country shillings. He was sober and reliable, with intense self-respect and a decided talent for the management of money. It was principally for this reason that he took great delight in his sudden wealth by legacy. He had thereby greater opportunities for the exercise of his native **shrewdness** in a bargain. This he **evinced** in his purchase of a house in Boston.

One day in spring the old Townsend house was shut up, the Blue Leopard was taken carefully down from his **lair** over the front door, the fam-

familiars *(noun)* household members

congregate[d] *(verb)* to gather; to assemble in a group

melancholy *(noun)* a depressed mood

evident *(adjective)* clear in terms of understanding

flaunt[ing] *(verb)* to display in an obnoxious manner; to show off

disparaging *(adjective)* negative; degrading

ily possessions were loaded on the train, and the Townsends departed. It was a sad and eventful day for Townsend Center. A man from Barre had rented the store—David had decided at the last not to sell—and the old **familiars congregated** in **melancholy** fashion and talked over the situation. An enormous pride over their departed townsman became **evident**. They paraded him, **flaunting** him like a banner in the eyes of the new man. "David is awful smart," they said; "there won't nobody get the better of him in the city if he has lived in Townsend Center all his life. He's got his eyes open. Know what he paid for his house in Boston? Well, sir, that house cost twenty-five thousand dollars, and David he bought it for five. Yes, sir, he did."

"Must have been some out about it," remarked the new man, scowling over his counter. He was beginning to feel his **disparaging** situation.

"Not an out, sir. David he made sure on't. Catch him gettin' bit. Everythin' was in apple-pie order, hot an' cold water and all, and in one of the best locations of the city—real high-up street. David he said the rent in that street was never under a

desirableness *(noun)* attractiveness

secure[d] *(verb)* to gain possession
ascertain[ed] *(verb)* to discover; to find out

amiss *(adjective)* flawed; incorrect

commence[d] *(verb)* to begin

allay[ed] *(verb)* to quiet; to reduce

thousand. Yes, sir, David he got a bargain—five thousand dollars for a twenty-five-thousand-dollar house."

"Some out about it!" growled the new man over the counter.

However, as his fellow townsmen and allies stated, there seemed to be no doubt about the **desirableness** of the city house which David Townsend had purchased and the fact that he had **secured** it for an absurdly low price. The whole family were at first suspicious. It was **ascertained** that the house had cost a round sum only a few years ago; it was in perfect repair; nothing whatever was **amiss** with plumbing, furnace, anything. There was not even a soap factory within smelling distance, as Mrs. Townsend had vaguely surmised. She was sure that she had heard of houses being undesirable for such reasons, but there was no soap factory. They all sniffed and peeked; when the first rainfall came they looked at the ceiling, confidently expecting to see dark spots where the leaks had **commenced**, but there were none. They were forced to confess that their suspicions were **allayed**, that the house was perfect, even over-

thrift *(noun)* strong concern for saving money

somewhat *(adverb)* to a degree; slightly

genteel *(adjective)* elegant; stylish
antecedents *(noun)* previous condition

singular *(adjective)* strange; unusual

shadowed with the mystery of a lower price than it was worth. That, however, was an additional perfection in the opinion of the Townsends, who had their share of New England **thrift**. They had lived just one month in their new house, and were happy, although at times **somewhat** lonely from missing the society of Townsend Center, when the trouble began. The Townsends, although they lived in a fine house in a **genteel**, almost fashionable, part of the city, were true to their **antecedents** and kept, as they had been accustomed, only one maid. She was the daughter of a farmer on the outskirts of their native village, was middle-aged, and had lived with them for the last ten years. One pleasant Monday morning she rose early and did the family washing before breakfast, which had been prepared by Mrs. Townsend and Adrianna, as was their habit on washing-days. The family were seated at the breakfast table in their basement dining-room, and this maid, whose name was Cordelia, was hanging out the clothes in the vacant lot. This vacant lot seemed a valuable one, being on a corner. It was rather **singular** that it had not been built upon. The Townsends had

utilize[d] *(verb)* to use
disregard *(noun)* to ignore; to neglect

regard[ing] *(verb)* to look at
countenance *(noun)* facial expression
indicative *(adjective)* serving to point out or to show
sodden *(adjective)* soaked with
bristle *(verb)* to become stiff or rigid

wondered at it and agreed that they would have preferred their own house to be there. They had, however, **utilized** it as far as possible with their innocent, rural **disregard** of property rights in unoccupied land.

"We might just as well hang out our washing in that vacant lot," Mrs. Townsend had told Cordelia the first Monday of their stay in the house. "Our little yard ain't half big enough for all our clothes, and it is sunnier there, too."

So Cordelia had hung out the wash there for four Mondays, and this was the fifth. The breakfast was about half finished—they had reached the buckwheat cakes—when this maid came rushing into the dining-room and stood **regarding** them, speechless, with a **countenance indicative** of the utmost horror. She was deadly pale. Her hands, **sodden** with soapsuds, hung twitching at her sides in the folds of her calico gown; her very hair, which was light and sparse, seemed to **bristle** with fear. All the Townsends turned and looked at her. David and George rose with a half-defined idea of burglars.

"Cordelia Battles, what is the matter?" cried

preemptory *(adjective)* intended to stall or prevent something

struck dumb *(idiom)* to be unable to speak

rousing *(adjective)* exciting; stirring
indignation *(noun)* anger; rage
proprietorship *(noun)* ownership

Mrs. Townsend. Adrianna gasped for breath and turned as white as the maid. "What is the matter?" repeated Mrs. Townsend, but the maid was unable to speak. Mrs. Townsend, who could be **preemptory**, sprang up, ran to the frightened woman and shook her violently. "Cordelia Battles, you speak," said she, "and not stand there staring that way, as if you were **struck dumb**! What is the matter with you?"

Then Cordelia spoke in a fainting voice.

"There's—somebody else—hanging out clothes—in the vacant lot," she gasped, and clutched at a chair for support.

"Who?" cried Mrs. Townsend, **rousing** to **indignation**, for already she had assumed a **proprietorship** in the vacant lot. "Is it the folks in the next house? I'd like to know what right they have! We are next to that vacant lot."

"I—dunno—who it is," gasped Cordelia.

"Why, we've seen that girl next door go to mass every morning," said Mrs. Townsend. "She's got a fiery red head. Seems as if you might know her by this time, Cordelia."

"It ain't that girl," gasped Cordelia. Then she

hesitate[d] *(verb)* to pause
utmost *(adjective)* most extreme; greatest

queer *(adjective)* odd; abnormal

added in a horror-stricken voice, "I couldn't see who 'twas."

They all stared.

"Why couldn't you see?" demanded her mistress. "Are you struck blind?"

"No, ma'am."

"Then why couldn't you see?"

"All I could see was—" Cordelia **hesitated**, with an expression of the **utmost** horror.

"Go on," said Mrs. Townsend, impatiently.

"All I could see was the shadow of somebody, very slim, hanging out the clothes, and—"

"What?"

"I could see the shadows of the things flappin' on their line."

"You couldn't see the clothes?"

"Only the shadow on the ground."

"What kind of clothes were they?"

"**Queer**," replied Cordelia, with a shudder.

"If I didn't know you so well, I should think you had been drinking," said Mrs. Townsend. "Now, Cordelia Battles, I'm going out in that vacant lot and see myself what you're talking about."

"I can't go," gasped the woman.

sally [ied] *(verb)* to rush forward

twinkle[d] *(verb)* to flutter
coarse *(adjective)* rough; harsh

rude *(adjective)* primitive; raw

exceedingly *(adverb)* to an extreme degree

nondescript *(adjective)* described with difficulty; unremarkable

strive [strove] *(verb)* to attempt; to struggle

With that Mrs. Townsend and all the others, except Adrianna, who remained to tremble with the maid, **sallied** forth into the vacant lot. They had to go out the area gate into the street to reach it. It was nothing unusual in the way of vacant lots. One large poplar tree, the relic of the old forest which had once flourished there, **twinkled** in one corner; for the rest, it was overgrown with **coarse** weeds and a few dusty flowers. The Townsends stood just inside the **rude** board fence which divided the lot from the street and stared with wonder and horror, for Cordelia had told the truth. They all saw what she had described—the shadow of an **exceedingly** slim woman moving along the ground with up-stretched arms, the shadows of strange, **nondescript** garments flapping from a shadowy line, but when they looked up for the substance of the shadows nothing was to be seen except the clear, blue October air.

"My goodness!" gasped Mrs. Townsend. Her face assumed a strange gathering of wrath in the midst of her terror. Suddenly she made a determined move forward, although her husband **strove** to hold her back.

recoil[ed] *(verb)* to move physically away or back

staunch *(adjective)* faithful; loyal
actualities *(noun)* realities; facts

convulsively *(adverb)* in a determined or decisive manner

"You let me be," said she. She moved forward. Then she **recoiled** and gave a loud shriek. "The wet sheet flapped in my face," she cried. "Take me away, take me away!" Then she fainted. Between them they got her back to the house. "It was awful," she moaned when she came to herself, with the family all around her where she lay on the dining-room floor. "Oh, David, what do you suppose it is?"

"Nothing at all," replied David Townsend stoutly. He was remarkable for courage and **staunch** belief in **actualities**. He was now denying to himself that he had seen anything unusual.

"Oh, there was," moaned his wife.

"I saw something," said George, in a sullen, boyish bass.

The maid sobbed **convulsively** and so did Adrianna for sympathy.

"We won't talk any about it," said David. "Here, Jane, you drink this hot tea—it will do you good; and Cordelia, you hang out the clothes in our own yard. George, you go and put up the line for her."

"The line is out there," said George, with a jerk of his shoulder.

resentfully *(adverb)* in a spastic or fitful manner

tumbler *(noun)* a container for liquid
slop[ped] *(verb)* to spill

"Are you afraid?"

"No, I ain't," replied the boy **resentfully**, and went out with a pale face.

After that Cordelia hung the Townsend wash in the yard of their own house, standing always with her back to the vacant lot. As for David Townsend, he spent a good deal of his time in the lot watching the shadows, but he came to no explanation, although he strove to satisfy himself with many.

"I guess the shadows come from the smoke from our chimneys, or else the poplar tree," he said.

"Why do the shadows come on Monday mornings, and no other?" demanded his wife.

David was silent.

Very soon new mysteries arose. One day Cordelia rang the dinner-bell at their usual dinner hour, the same as in Townsend Center high noon, and the family assembled. With amazement Adrianna looked at the dishes on the table.

"Why, that's queer!" she said.

"What's queer?" asked her mother.

Cordelia stopped short as she was about setting a **tumbler** of water beside a plate, and the water **slopped** over.

pallor *(noun)* paleness; the absence of color

exclamation *(noun)* a loud and sudden statement

reluctantly *(adverb)* in a hesitant or unwilling manner

"Why," said Adrianna, her face paling, "I—thought there was boiled dinner. I—smelt cabbage cooking."

"I knew there would something else come up," gasped Cordelia, leaning hard on the back of Adrianna's chair.

"What do you mean?" asked Mrs. Townsend sharply, but her own face began to assume the shocked **pallor** which it was so easy nowadays for all their faces to assume at the merest suggestion of anything out of the common.

"I smelt cabbage cooking all the morning up in my room," Adrianna said faintly, "and here's codfish and potatoes for dinner."

The Townsends all looked at one another. David rose with an **exclamation** and rushed out of the room. The others waited tremblingly. When he came back his face was lowering.

"What did you—" Mrs. Townsend asked hesitatingly.

"There's some smell of cabbage out there," he admitted **reluctantly**. Then he looked at her with a challenge. "It comes from the next house," he said. "Blows over our house."

account for *(idiom)* explain

switch[ed] *(verb)* to move; to whisk
set hard *(idiom)* unmoving

conclusive *(adjective)* decisive; definitive

"Our house is higher."

"I don't care; you can never **account for** such things."

"Cordelia," said Mrs. Townsend, "you go over to the next house and you ask if they've got cabbage for dinner."

Cordelia **switched** out of the room, her mouth **set hard**. She came back promptly.

"Says they never have cabbage," she announced with gloomy triumph and a **conclusive** glance at Mr. Townsend. "Their girl was real sassy."

"Oh, father, let's move away; let's sell the house," cried Adrianna in a panic-stricken tone.

"If you think I'm going to sell a house that I got as cheap as this one because we smell cabbage in a vacant lot, you're mistaken," replied David firmly.

"It isn't the cabbage alone," said Mrs. Townsend.

"And a few shadows," added David. "I am tired of such nonsense. I thought you had more sense, Jane."

"One of the boys at school asked me if we lived in the house next to the vacant lot on Wells Street and whistled when I said 'Yes,'" remarked George.

stimulated *(adjective)* aroused; provoked

twilight *(noun)* the time between sunset and night

"Let him whistle," said Mr. Townsend.

After a few hours the family, **stimulated** by Mr. Townsend's calm, common sense, agreed that it was exceedingly foolish to be disturbed by a mysterious odor of cabbage. They even laughed at themselves.

"I suppose we have got so nervous over those shadows hanging out clothes that we notice every little thing," conceded Mrs. Townsend.

"You will find out some day that that is no more to be regarded than the cabbage," said her husband.

"You can't account for that wet sheet hitting my face," said Mrs. Townsend, doubtfully.

"You imagined it."

"I FELT it."

That afternoon things went on as usual in the household until nearly four o'clock. Adrianna went downtown to do some shopping. Mrs. Townsend sat sewing beside the bay window in her room, which was a front one in the third story. George had not got home. Mr. Townsend was writing a letter in the library. Cordelia was busy in the basement; the **twilight**, which was coming earlier

gather *(verb)* to increase; to accumulate

looking-glass *(noun)* mirror
simultaneously *(adverb)* occurring at the same moment in time
shiver[ed] *(verb)* to shatter
fragments *(noun)* broken pieces

incredulous *(adjective)* disbelieving; skeptical

inexpressibly *(adverb)* in a manner that is difficult to express

inconsequently *(adverb)* in an irrelevant manner

and earlier every night, was beginning to **gather,** when suddenly there was a loud crash which shook the house from its foundations. Even the dishes on the sideboard rattled, and the glasses rang like bells. The pictures on the walls of Mrs. Townsend's room swung out from the walls. But that was not all: every **looking-glass** in the house cracked **simultaneously**—as nearly as they could judge—from top to bottom, then **shivered** into **fragments** over the floors. Mrs. Townsend was too frightened to scream. She sat huddled in her chair, gasping for breath, her eyes, rolling from side to side in **incredulous** terror, turned toward the street. She saw a great black group of people crossing it just in front of the vacant lot. There was something **inexpressibly** strange and gloomy about this moving group; there was an effect of sweeping, wavings and foldings of sable draperies and gleams of deadly white faces; then they passed. She twisted her head to see, and they disappeared in the vacant lot. Mr. Townsend came hurrying into the room; he was pale, and looked at once angry and alarmed.

"Did you fall?" he asked **inconsequently**, as if his

manifestation *(noun)* example of power

reel[ed] *(verb)* to move in an unsteady manner
sideways glance *(idiom)* a disapproving look
commiserate[ing] *(verb)* to feel sympathy with
or condolence for

wife, who was small, could have produced such a **manifestation** by a fall.

"Oh, David, what is it?" whispered Mrs. Townsend.

"Darned if I know!" said David.

"Don't swear. It's too awful. Oh, see the looking-glass, David!"

"I see it. The one over the library mantel is broken, too."

"Oh, it is a sign of death!"

Cordelia's feet were heard as she staggered on the stairs. She almost fell into the room. She **reeled** over to Mr. Townsend and clutched his arm. He cast a **sidewise glance**, half furious, half **commiserating** at her.

"Well, what is it all about?" he asked.

"I don't know. What is it? Oh, what is it? The looking-glass in the kitchen is broken. All over the floor. Oh, oh! What is it?"

"I don't know any more than you do. I didn't do it."

"Lookin'-glasses broken is a sign of death in the house," said Cordelia. "If it's me, I hope I'm ready; but I'd rather die than be so scared as I've been lately."

shook himself loose *(idiom)* freed himself
eye[d] *(verb)* to look at closely
gathering *(adjective)* increasing; accumulating
resolution *(noun)* resolve; courage

rigid *(adjective)* stiff
converge[d] *(verb)* to meet; to come together

gruesome *(adjective)* horrifying; ghastly

Mr. Townsend **shook himself loose** and **eyed** the two trembling women with **gathering resolution**.

"Now, look here, both of you," he said. "This is nonsense. You'll die sure enough of fright if you keep on this way. I was a fool myself to be startled. Everything it is is an earthquake."

"Oh, David!" gasped his wife, not much reassured.

"It is nothing but an earthquake," persisted Mr. Townsend. "It acted just like that. Things always are broken on the walls, and the middle of the room isn't affected. I've read about it."

Suddenly Mrs. Townsend gave a loud shriek and pointed.

"How do you account for that," she cried, "if it's an earthquake? Oh, oh, oh!"

She was on the verge of hysterics. Her husband held her firmly by the arm as his eyes followed the direction of her **rigid** pointing finger. Cordelia looked also, her eyes seeming **converged** to a bright point of fear. On the floor in front of the broken looking-glass lay a mass of black stuff in a **gruesome** long ridge.

stride *(noun)* step

imbued *(adjective)* filled; permeated

resentful *(adjective)* full of negative feelings

heap *(noun)* pile

racking *(adjective)* torturous; violent

"It's something you dropped there," almost shouted Mr. Townsend.

"It ain't. Oh!"

Mr. Townsend dropped his wife's arm and took one **stride** toward the object. It was a very long crape veil. He lifted it, and it floated out from his arm as if **imbued** with electricity.

"It's yours," he said to his wife.

"Oh, David, I never had one. You know, oh, you know I—shouldn't—unless you died. How came it there?"

"I'm darned if I know," said David, regarding it. He was deadly pale, but still **resentful** rather than afraid.

"Don't hold it; don't!"

"I'd like to know what in thunder all this means?" said David. He gave the thing an angry toss and it fell on the floor in exactly the same long **heap** as before.

Cordelia began to weep with **racking** sobs. Mrs. Townsend reached out and caught her husband's hand, clutching it hard with ice-cold fingers.

"What's got into this house, anyhow?" he growled.

suspended *(adjective)* hanging; dangling
pursue[d] *(verb)* to chase
clutch[ing] *(verb)* to hold; to grasp
vainly *(adverb)* in a useless or futile manner
hurrying *(adjective)* rapidly moving

unintelligibly *(adverb)* in a manner that makes
    no sense

"You'll have to sell it. Oh, David, we can't live here."

"As for my selling a house I paid only five thousand for when it's worth twenty-five, for any such nonsense as this, I won't!"

David gave one stride toward the black veil, but it rose from the floor and moved away before him across the room at exactly the same height as if **suspended** from a woman's head. He **pursued** it, **clutching vainly**, all around the room, then he swung himself on his heel with an exclamation and the thing fell to the floor again in the long heap. Then were heard **hurrying** feet on the stairs and Adrianna burst into the room. She ran straight to her father and clutched his arm; she tried to speak, but she chattered **unintelligibly**; her face was blue. Her father shook her violently.

"Adrianna, do have more sense!" he cried.

"Oh, David, how can you talk so?" sobbed her mother.

"I can't help it. I'm mad!" said he with emphasis. "What has got into this house and you all, anyhow?"

"What is it, Adrianna, poor child," asked her

engrossed *(adjective)* consumed; occupied

feebly *(adverb)* in a weak manner

mad *(adjective)* crazy; insane

mother. "Only look what has happened here."

"It's an earthquake," said her father staunchly; "nothing to be afraid of."

"How do you account for THAT?" said Mrs. Townsend in an awful voice, pointing to the veil.

Adrianna did not look—she was too **engrossed** with her own terrors. She began to speak in a breathless voice.

"I—was—coming—by the vacant lot," she panted, "and—I—I—had my new hat in a paper bag and— a parcel of blue ribbon, and—I saw a crowd, an awful—oh! a whole crowd of people with white faces, as if—they were dressed all in black."

"Where are they now?"

"I don't know. Oh!" Adrianna sank gasping **feebly** into a chair.

"Get her some water, David," sobbed her mother.

David rushed with an impatient exclamation out of the room and returned with a glass of water which he held to his daughter's lips.

"Here, drink this!" he said roughly.

"Oh, David, how can you speak so?" sobbed his wife.

"I can't help it. I'm **mad** clean through," said David.

unconcern *(noun)* indifference; a lack of worry

screech[ed] *(verb)* a sharp yell or scream

daresay *(verb)* to think something true; to agree

Then there was a hard bound upstairs, and George entered. He was very white, but he grinned at them with an appearance of **unconcern**.

"Hullo!" he said in a shaking voice, which he tried to control. "What on earth's to pay in that vacant lot now?"

"Well, what is it?" demanded his father.

"Oh, nothing, only—well, there are lights over it exactly as if there was a house there, just about where the windows would be. It looked as if you could walk right in, but when you look close there are those old dried-up weeds rattling away on the ground the same as ever. I looked at it and couldn't believe my eyes. A woman saw it, too. She came along just as I did. She gave one look, then she **screeched** and ran. I waited for some one else, but nobody came."

Mr. Townsend rushed out of the room.

"I **daresay** it'll be gone when he gets there," began George, then he stared round the room. "What's to pay here?" he cried.

"Oh, George, the whole house shook all at once, and all the looking-glasses broke," wailed his mother, and Adrianna and Cordelia joined.

stood just about enough *(idiom)* tolerated
  enough

egress *(noun)* exit
hurriedly *(adverb)* in a rushed manner

George whistled with pale lips. Then Mr. Townsend entered.

"Well," asked George, "see anything?"

"I don't want to talk," said his father. "I've **stood just about enough.**"

"We've got to sell out and go back to Townsend Center," cried his wife in a wild voice. "Oh, David, say you'll go back."

"I won't go back for any such nonsense as this, and sell a twenty-five thousand dollar house for five thousand," said he firmly.

But that very night his resolution was shaken. The whole family watched together in the dining-room. They were all afraid to go to bed—that is, all except possibly Mr. Townsend. Mrs. Townsend declared firmly that she for one would leave that awful house and go back to Townsend Center whether he came or not, unless they all stayed together and watched, and Mr. Townsend yielded. They chose the dining-room for the reason that it was nearer the street should they wish to make their **egress hurriedly**, and they took up their station around the dining-table on which Cordelia had placed a luncheon.

ostentatiously *(adverb)* in an overly showy
manner
rove[ing] *(verb)* to wander; to move
comparing notes *(idiom)* as if trying to find
similarities
furtively *(adverb)* in a secretive manner

radiance *(noun)* glowing light

"It looks exactly as if we were watching with a corpse," she said in a horror-stricken whisper.

"Hold your tongue if you can't talk sense," said Mr. Townsend.

The dining-room was very large, finished in oak, with a dark blue paper above the wainscotting. The old sign of the tavern, the Blue Leopard, hung over the mantel-shelf. Mr. Townsend had insisted on hanging it there. He had a curious pride in it. The family sat together until after midnight and nothing unusual happened. Mrs. Townsend began to nod; Mr. Townsend read the paper **ostentatiously**. Adrianna and Cordelia stared with **roving** eyes about the room, then at each other as if **comparing notes** on terror. George had a book which he studied **furtively**. All at once Adrianna gave a startled exclamation and Cordelia echoed her. George whistled faintly. Mrs. Townsend awoke with a start and Mr. Townsend's paper rattled to the floor.

"Look!" gasped Adrianna.

The sign of the Blue Leopard over the shelf glowed as if a lantern hung over it. The **radiance** was

transfixed *(adjective)* motionless

accord *(noun)* unplanned intention to act

trifle *(noun)* a small degree

ply[ing] *(verb)* to use

thrown from above. It grew brighter and brighter as they watched. The Blue Leopard seemed to crouch and spring with life. Then the door into the front hall opened—the outer door, which had been carefully locked. It squeaked and they all recognized it. They sat staring. Mr. Townsend was as **transfixed** as the rest. They heard the outer door shut, then the door into the room swung open and slowly that awful black group of people which they had seen in the afternoon entered. The Townsends with one **accord** rose and huddled together in a far corner; they all held to each other and stared. The people, their faces gleaming with a whiteness of death, their black robes waving and folding, crossed the room. They were a **trifle** above mortal height, or seemed so to the terrified eyes which saw them. They reached the mantel-shelf where the sign-board hung, then a black-draped long arm was seen to rise and make a motion, as if **plying** a knocker. Then the whole company passed out of sight, as if through the wall, and the room was as before. Mrs. Townsend was shaking in a nervous chill, Adrianna was almost fainting, Cordelia was in hysterics. David

clear[ed] *(verb)* to become clear

mutter[ed] *(verb)* to say something without speaking clearly or loudly

sharply *(adverb)* in a harsh manner

Townsend stood glaring in a curious way at the sign of the Blue Leopard. George stared at him with a look of horror. There was something in his father's face which made him forget everything else. At last he touched his arm timidly.

"Father," he whispered.

David turned and regarded him with a look of rage and fury, then his face **cleared**; he passed his hand over his forehead.

"Good Lord! What DID come to me?" he **muttered**.

"You looked like that awful picture of old Tom Townsend in the garret in Townsend Center, father," whimpered the boy, shuddering.

"Should think I might look like 'most any old cuss after such darned work as this," growled David, but his face was white. "Go and pour out some hot tea for your mother," he ordered the boy **sharply**. He himself shook Cordelia violently. "Stop such actions!" he shouted in her ears, and shook her again. "Ain't you a church member?" he demanded; "what be you afraid of? You ain't done nothin' wrong, have ye?"

iniquity *(noun)* sin; wickedness

liable *(adjective)* responsible
shrill *(adjective)* piercing; high-pitched

spasmodic *(adjective)* fitful; jerky

conclusively *(adverb)* in a decisive or definitive
   manner

Then Cordelia quoted Scripture in a burst of sobs and laughter.

"Behold, I was shapen in **iniquity**; and in sin did my mother conceive me," she cried out. "If I ain't done wrong, maybe them that's come before me did, and when the Evil One and the Powers of Darkness is abroad I'm **liable**, I'm liable!" Then she laughed loud and long and **shrill**.

"If you don't hush up," said David, but still with that white terror and horror on his own face, "I'll bundle you out in that vacant lot whether or no. I mean it."

Then Cordelia was quiet, after one wild roll of her eyes at him. The color was returning to Adrianna's cheeks; her mother was drinking hot tea in **spasmodic** gulps.

"It's after midnight," she gasped, "and I don't believe they'll come again to-night. Do you, David?"

"No, I don't," said David **conclusively**.

"Oh, David, we mustn't stay another night in this awful house."

suspect[ed] *(verb)* to doubt; to distrust

inquiry[ies] *(noun)* a question or request for more information

"We won't. To-morrow we'll pack off bag and baggage to Townsend Center, if it takes all the fire department to move us," said David.

Adrianna smiled in the midst of her terror. She thought of Abel Lyons.

The next day Mr. Townsend went to the real estate agent who had sold him the house.

"It's no use," he said, "I can't stand it. Sell the house for what you can get. I'll give it away rather than keep it."

Then he added a few strong words as to his opinion of parties who sold him such an establishment. But the agent pleaded innocent for the most part.

"I'll own I **suspected** something wrong when the owner, who pledged me to secrecy as to his name, told me to sell that place for what I could get, and did not limit me. I had never heard anything, but I began to suspect something was wrong. Then I made a few **inquiries** and found out that there was a rumor in the neighbourhood that there was something out of the usual about that vacant lot. I had wondered myself why it wasn't built upon. There was a story about it's being undertaken

timid *(adjective)* fearful; not brave

flourish[ed] *(verb)* to be active; to be prosperous

once, and the contract made, and the contractor dying; then another man took it and one of the workmen was killed on his way to dig the cellar, and the others struck. I didn't pay much attention to it. I never believed much in that sort of thing anyhow, and then, too, I couldn't find out that there had ever been anything wrong about the house itself, except as the people who had lived there were said to have seen and heard queer things in the vacant lot, so I thought you might be able to get along, especially as you didn't look like a man who was **timid,** and the house was such a bargain as I never handled before. But this you tell me is beyond belief."

"Do you know the names of the people who formerly owned the vacant lot?" asked Mr. Townsend.

"I don't know for certain," replied the agent, "for the original owners **flourished** long before your or my day, but I do know that the lot goes by the name of the old Gaston lot. What's the matter? Are you ill?"

urbanely *(adverb)* in a polite, elegant manner

"No; it is nothing," replied Mr. Townsend. "Get what you can for the house; perhaps another family might not be as troubled as we have been."

"I hope you are not going to leave the city?" said the agent, **urbanely.**

"I am going back to Townsend Center as fast as steam can carry me after we get packed up and out of that cursed house," replied Mr. David Townsend.

He did not tell the agent nor any of his family what had caused him to start when told the name of the former owners of the lot. He remembered all at once the story of a ghastly murder which had taken place in the Blue Leopard. The victim's name was Gaston and the murderer had never been discovered.

illuminated *(adjective)* lit up; filled with light
failing *(adjective)* weakening; dying
gravely *(adverb)* in a serious manner

controvert[ed] *(verb)* to oppose

moreover *(adverb)* besides; in addition

arms *(noun)* weapons
imply *(verb)* to suggest; to say indirectly

The Stranger

by Ambrose Bierce

A man stepped out of the darkness into the little **illuminated** circle about our **failing** campfire and seated himself upon a rock.

"You are not the first to explore this region," he said, **gravely.**

Nobody **controverted** his statement; he was himself proof of its truth, for he was not of our party and must have been somewhere near when we camped. **Moreover,** he must have companions not far away; it was not a place where one would be living or traveling alone. For more than a week we had seen, besides ourselves and our animals, only such living things as rattlesnakes and horned toads. In an Arizona desert one does not long coexist with only such creatures as these: one must have pack animals, supplies, **arms**—"an outfit." And all these **imply** comrades. It was perhaps a doubt as to what manner of men this

unceremonious *(adjective)* informal
interpretable *(adjective)* able to be explained

posture *(noun)* position of the body

deliberate *(adjective)* intentional
uninflected *(adjective)* unchanging

due west *(idiom)* in a westerly direction
configuration *(noun)* shape; arrangement
prospect[ing] *(verb)* to explore; to inspect
intention *(noun)* purpose; objective

unceremonious stranger's comrades might be, together with something in his words **interpretable** as a challenge, that caused every man of our half-dozen "gentlemen adventurers" to rise to a sitting **posture** and lay his hand upon a weapon—an act signifying, in that time and place, a policy of expectation. The stranger gave the matter no attention and began again to speak in the same **deliberate**, **uninflected** monotone in which he had delivered his first sentence:

"Thirty years ago Ramon Gallegos, William Shaw, George W. Kent and Berry Davis, all of Tucson, crossed the Santa Catalina mountains and traveled **due west**, as nearly as the **configuration** of the country permitted. We were **prospecting** and it was our **intention**, if we found nothing, to push through to the Gila river at some point near Big Bend, where we understood there was a settlement. We had a good outfit but no guide—just Ramon Gallegos, William Shaw, George W. Kent and Berry Davis."

The man repeated the names slowly and distinctly, as if to fix them in the memories of his audience, every member of which was now

slackened *(adjective)* lessening; decreasing
apprehension *(noun)* fear

solitary *(noun)* lonely; isolated
had a tendency *(idiom)* to be likely to

aberration *(noun)* disorder

generic *(adjective)* indistinct; general

torsions *(noun)* twisting forces

witless *(adjective)* crazy; foolish

undertake *(verb)* to attempt

attentively observing him, but with a **slackened apprehension** regarding his possible companions somewhere in the darkness that seemed to enclose us like a black wall; in the manner of this volunteer historian was no suggestion of an unfriendly purpose. His act was rather that of a harmless lunatic than an enemy. We were not so new to the country as not to know that the **solitary** life of many a plainsman **had a tendency** to develop eccentricities of conduct and character not always easily distinguishable from mental **aberration**. A man is like a tree: in a forest of his fellows he will grow as straight as his **generic** and individual nature permits; alone in the open, he yields to the deforming stresses and **torsions** that environ him. Some such thoughts were in my mind as I watched the man from the shadow of my hat, pulled low to shut out the firelight. A **witless** fellow, no doubt, but what could he be doing there in the heart of a desert?

Having **undertaken** to tell this story, I wish that I could describe the man's appearance; that would be a natural thing to do. Unfortunately, and somewhat strangely, I find myself unable to do so with

elude *(verb)* to escape; to avoid

infrequent *(adjective)* not occurring often

expedition *(noun)* a journey with a specific purpose

alter[ed] *(verb)* to change

intolerable *(adjective)* unbearable; extreme

casks *(noun)* barrel or container

any degree of confidence, for afterward no two of us agreed as to what he wore and how he looked; and when I try to set down my own impressions they **elude** me. Anyone can tell some kind of story; narration is one of the elemental powers of the race. But the talent for description is a gift.

Nobody having broken silence the visitor went on to say:

"This country was not then what it is now. There was not a ranch between the Gila and the Gulf. There was a little game here and there in the mountains, and near the **infrequent** water-holes grass enough to keep our animals from starvation. If we should be so fortunate as to encounter no Indians we might get through. But within a week the purpose of the **expedition** had **altered** from discovery of wealth to preservation of life. We had gone too far to go back, for what was ahead could be no worse than what was behind; so we pushed on, riding by night to avoid Indians and the **intolerable** heat, and concealing ourselves by day as best we could. Sometimes, having exhausted our supply of wild meat and emptied our **casks**, we were days without food or drink; then a water-

arroyo *(noun)* a channel created due to the flow of water

restore[d] *(verb)* to renew; to return

skirt[ed] *(verb)* to go around

practicable *(adjective)* usable

pass *(noun)* a path through a barrier

gulch *(noun)* ravine

urge[d] *(verb)* to stimulate; to compel

footing *(noun)* a position where a foot can be placed

hole or a shallow pool in the bottom of an **arroyo** so **restored** our strength and sanity that we were able to shoot some of the wild animals that sought it also. Sometimes it was a bear, sometimes an antelope, a coyote, a cougar—that was as God pleased; all were food.

"One morning as we **skirted** a mountain range, seeking a **practicable pass**, we were attacked by a band of Apaches who had followed our trail up a **gulch**—it is not far from here. Knowing that they outnumbered us ten to one, they took none of their usual cowardly precautions, but dashed upon us at a gallop, firing and yelling. Fighting was out of the question: we **urged** our feeble animals up the gulch as far as there was **footing** for a hoof, then threw ourselves out of our saddles and took to the chaparral on one of the slopes, abandoning our entire outfit to the enemy. But we retained our rifles, every man—Ramon Gallegos, William Shaw, George W. Kent and Berry Davis."

"Same old crowd," said the humorist of our party. He was an Eastern man, unfamiliar with the decent observances of social intercourse. A gesture of disapproval from our leader silenced him

cutting off *(idiom)* preventing

vertical *(adjective)* up and down; upright

cavern *(noun)* a large cave

sortie *(noun)* an attack from the defensive position

and the stranger proceeded with his tale:

"The savages dismounted also, and some of them ran up the gulch beyond the point at which we had left it, **cutting off** further retreat in that direction and forcing us on up the side. Unfortunately the chaparral extended only a short distance up the slope, and as we came into the open ground above we took the fire of a dozen rifles; but Apaches shoot badly when in a hurry, and God so willed it that none of us fell. Twenty yards up the slope, beyond the edge of the brush, were **vertical** cliffs, in which, directly in front of us, was a narrow opening. Into that we ran, finding ourselves in a **cavern** about as large as an ordinary room in a house. Here for a time we were safe: a single man with a repeating rifle could defend the entrance against all the Apaches in the land. But against hunger and thirst we had no defense. Courage we still had, but hope was a memory.

"Not one of those Indians did we afterward see, but by the smoke and glare of their fires in the gulch we knew that by day and by night they watched with ready rifles in the edge of the bush—knew that if we made a **sortie** not a man of

in turn *(idiom)* taking turns

insupportable *(adjective)* not able to be endured

mad *(adjective)* crazy; insane

in bad taste *(idiom)* against people's preferences

us would live to take three steps into the open. For three days, watching **in turn**, we held out before our suffering became **insupportable**. Then—it was the morning of the fourth day—Ramon Gallegos said:

"'Senores, I know not well of the good God and what please him. I have live without religion, and I am not acquaint with that of you. Pardon, senores, if I shock you, but for me the time is come to beat the game of the Apache.'

"He knelt upon the rock floor of the cave and pressed his pistol against his temple. 'Madre de Dios,' he said, 'comes now the soul of Ramon Gallegos.'

"And so he left us—William Shaw, George W. Kent and Berry Davis.

"I was the leader: it was for me to speak.

"'He was a brave man,' I said—'he knew when to die, and how. It is foolish to go **mad** from thirst and fall by Apache bullets, or be skinned alive—it is **in bad taste**. Let us join Ramon Gallegos.'"

"'That is right,' said William Shaw.

"'That is right,' said George W. Kent.

"I straightened the limbs of Ramon Gallegos and

commotion *(noun)* disturbance; confusion
spring [sprung] *(verb)* to leap

put a handkerchief over his face. Then William Shaw said: 'I should like to look like that—a little while.'

"And George W. Kent said that he felt that way, too.

"'It shall be so,' I said: 'the red devils will wait a week. William Shaw and George W. Kent, draw and kneel.'

"They did so and I stood before them.

"'Almighty God, our Father,' said I.

"'Almighty God, our Father,' said William Shaw.

"'Almighty God, our Father,' said George W. Kent.

"'Forgive us our sins,' said I.

"'Forgive us our sins,' said they.

"'And receive our souls.'

"'And receive our souls.'

"'Amen!'

"'Amen!'

"I laid them beside Ramon Gallegos and covered their faces."

There was a quick **commotion** on the opposite side of the campfire: one of our party had **sprung** to his feet, pistol in hand.

grasp[ing] *(verb)* to hold tightly; to clutch

inattentive *(adjective)* not mindful; not attentive
seize[d] *(verb)* to grasp; to clutch

insurgent *(noun)* rebel; revolutionary

scalped *(adjective)* missing the scalp from the
head
mutilated *(adjective)* to destroy; to maim

expiring *(adjective)* ending; dying

"And you!" he shouted—"YOU dared to escape?—you dare to be alive? You cowardly hound, I'll send you to join them if I hang for it!"

But with the leap of a panther the captain was upon him, **grasping** his wrist. "Hold it in, Sam Yountsey, hold it in!"

We were now all upon our feet—except the stranger, who sat motionless and apparently **inattentive**. Some one **seized** Yountsey's other arm.

"Captain," I said, "there is something wrong here. This fellow is either a lunatic or merely a liar—just a plain, every-day liar whom Yountsey has no call to kill. If this man was of that party it had five members, one of whom—probably himself—he has not named."

"Yes," said the captain, releasing the **insurgent**, who sat down, "there is something—unusual. Years ago four dead bodies of white men, **scalped** and shamefully **mutilated**, were found about the mouth of that cave. They are buried there; I have seen the graves—we shall all see them to-morrow."

The stranger rose, standing tall in the light of the **expiring** fire, which in our breathless atten-

reiterate[d] *(verb)* to state again for a second
   time; to repeat

strode [stride] *(verb)* to move; to walk

got on [to] my nerves *(idiom)* to be annoying

obediently *(adverb)* in a submissive manner

tion to his story we had neglected to keep going.

"There were four," he said—"Ramon Gallegos, William Shaw, George W. Kent and Berry Davis."

With this **reiterated** roll-call of the dead he walked into the darkness and we saw him no more.

At that moment one of our party, who had been on guard, **strode** in among us, rifle in hand and somewhat excited.

"Captain," he said, "for the last half-hour three men have been standing out there on the mesa." He pointed in the direction taken by the stranger. "I could see them distinctly, for the moon is up, but as they had no guns and I had them covered with mine I thought it was their move. They have made none, but, damn it! they have **got on to my nerves**."

"Go back to your post, and stay till you see them again," said the captain. "The rest of you lie down again, or I'll kick you all into the fire."

The sentinel **obediently** withdrew, swearing, and did not return. As we were arranging our blankets the fiery Yountsey said: "I beg your pardon, Captain, but who the devil do you take them to be?"

"Ramon Gallegos, William Shaw and George W. Kent."

"But how about Berry Davis? I ought to have shot him."

"Quite needless; you couldn't have made him any deader. Go to sleep."

prosper[ed] *(verb)* to succeed; to flourish
renew *(verb)* to resume; to begin anew

affection *(noun)* feeling; fondness
chief of these *(idiom)* the most important of
these; primarily
desultory *(adjective)* irregular
indisposition *(noun)* aversion; disinclination

scholarly *(adverb)* in a learned or academic
manner
aversion *(noun)* avoidance; feeling against

Beyond the Wall

by Ambrose Bierce

Many years ago, on my way from Hong Kong to New York, I passed a week in San Francisco. A long time had gone by since I had been in that city, during which my ventures in the Orient had **prospered** beyond my hope; I was rich and could afford to revisit my own country to **renew** my friendship with such of the companions of my youth as still lived and remembered me with the old **affection. Chief of these,** I hoped, was Mohun Dampier, an old schoolmate with whom I had held a **desultory** correspondence which had long ceased, as is the way of correspondence between men. You may have observed that the **indisposition** to write a merely social letter is in the ratio of the square of the distance between you and your correspondent. It is a law.

I remembered Dampier as a handsome, strong young fellow of **scholarly** tastes, with an **aversion**

singular *(adjective)* strange; unusual

perilous *(adjective)* dangerous
incursions *(noun)* raid; violent entrance into
realm *(noun)* domain
renounce[ing] *(verb)* to give up; to abandon
certitude *(noun)* certainty
incessant *(adjective)* unending; continual

hurl[ed] *(verb)* to throw; to thrust

sparsely *(adverb)* to a thin or meager degree

to work and a marked indifference to many of the things that the world cares for, including wealth, of which, however, he had inherited enough to put him beyond the reach of want. In his family, one of the oldest and most aristocratic in the country, it was, I think, a matter of pride that no member of it had ever been in trade nor politics, nor suffered any kind of distinction. Mohun was a trifle sentimental, and had in him a **singular** element of superstition, which led him to the study of all manner of occult subjects, although his sane mental health safeguarded him against fantastic **and perilous** faiths. He made daring **incursions** into the **realm** of the unreal without **renouncing** his residence in the partly surveyed and charted region of what we are pleased to call **certitude.**

The night of my visit to him was stormy. The Californian winter was on, and the **incessant** rain plashed in the deserted streets, or, lifted by irregular gusts of wind, was **hurled** against the houses with incredible fury. With no small difficulty my cabman found the right place, away out toward the ocean beach, in a **sparsely** populated suburb. The dwelling, a rather ugly one, apparently, stood

destitute *(adjective)* lacking possessions; in poverty

torment *(noun)* torture; agony

tempest *(noun)* storm

dismal *(adjective)* dreary; dreadful

rill *(noun)* a small stream

scuttle[d] *(verb)* to scurry; to move quickly

apprise[ing] *(verb)* to inform; to tell

accord[ed] *(verb)* to grant; to give

in the center of its grounds, which as nearly as I could make out in the gloom were **destitute** of either flowers or grass. Three or four trees, writhing and moaning in the **torment** of the **tempest**, appeared to be trying to escape from their **dismal** environment and take the chance of finding a better one out at sea. The house was a two-story brick structure with a tower, a story higher, at one corner. In a window of that was the only visible light. Something in the appearance of the place made me shudder, a performance that may have been assisted by a **rill** of rain-water down my back as I **scuttled** to cover in the doorway.

In answer to my note **apprising** him of my wish to call, Dampier had written, "Don't ring—open the door and come up." I did so. The staircase was dimly lighted by a single gas-jet at the top of the second flight. I managed to reach the landing without disaster and entered by an open door into the lighted square room of the tower. Dampier came forward in gown and slippers to receive me, giving me the greeting that I wished, and if I had held a thought that it might more fitly have been **accorded** me at the front door the first look at him

dispel[led] *(verb)* to scatter; to drive away

inhospitality *(noun)* unfriendliness; unwelcome feeling

pronounced *(adjective)* distinct; remarkable

stoop *(noun)* bending of the shoulders

angular *(adjective)* marked by harsh lines

uncanny *(adjective)* eerie; supernatural

sincerity *(noun)* honesty; purity

dominated *(adjective)* controlled; overwhelmed

dispelled any sense of his **inhospitality.**

He was not the same. Hardly past middle age, he had gone gray and had acquired a **pronounced stoop**. His figure was thin and **angular**, his face deeply lined, his complexion dead-white, without a touch of color. His eyes, unnaturally large, glowed with a fire that was almost **uncanny.**

He seated me, proffered a cigar, and with grave and obvious **sincerity** assured me of the pleasure that it gave him to meet me. Some unimportant conversation followed, but all the while I was **dominated** by a melancholy sense of the great change in him. This he must have perceived, for he suddenly said with a bright enough smile, "You are disappointed in me—non sum qualis eram."

I hardly knew what to reply, but managed to say: "Why, really, I don't know: your Latin is about the same."

He brightened again. "No," he said, "being a dead language, it grows in appropriateness. But please have the patience to wait: where I am going there is perhaps a better tongue. Will you care to have a message in it?"

The smile faded as he spoke, and as he con-

gravity *(noun)* seriousness

prescience *(noun)* foresight; knowledge of
    future events
cease *(verb)* to stop

dispiriting *(adjective)* lacking enthusiasm

startling *(adjective)* surprising; shocking

admittance *(noun)* entrance
assurance *(noun)* a guarantee; a pledge
adjoining *(adjective)* connected; adjacent

cluded he was looking into my eyes with a **gravity** that distressed me. Yet I would not surrender myself to his mood, nor permit him to see how deeply his **prescience** of death affected me.

"I fancy that it will be long," I said, "before human speech will **cease** to serve our need; and then the need, with its possibilities of service, will have passed."

He made no reply, and I too was silent, for the talk had taken a **dispiriting** turn, yet I knew not how to give it a more agreeable character. Suddenly, in a pause of the storm, when the dead silence was almost **startling** by contrast with the previous uproar, I heard a gentle tapping, which appeared to come from the wall behind my chair. The sound was such as might have been made by a human hand, not as upon a door by one asking **admittance**, but rather, I thought, as an agreed signal, an **assurance** of someone's presence in an **adjoining** room; most of us, I fancy, have had more experience of such communications than we should care to relate. I glanced at Dampier. If possibly there was something of amusement in the look he did not observe it. He appeared to

insistence *(noun)* urgency; impelling feeling

incomplete *(adjective)* unfinished

murk *(noun)* gloom; dreariness
torrents *(noun)* heavy outpouring

have forgotten my presence, and was staring at the wall behind me with an expression in his eyes that I am unable to name, although my memory of it is as vivid to-day as was my sense of it then. The situation was embarrassing; I rose to take my leave. At this he seemed to recover himself.

"Please be seated," he said; "it is nothing—no one is there."

But the tapping was repeated, and with the same gentle, slow **insistence** as before.

"Pardon me," I said, "it is late. May I call to-morrow?"

He smiled—a little mechanically, I thought. "It is very delicate of you," said he, "but quite needless. Really, this is the only room in the tower, and no one is there. At least—" He left the sentence **incomplete**, rose, and threw up a window, the only opening in the wall from which the sound seemed to come. "See."

Not clearly knowing what else to do I followed him to the window and looked out. A street-lamp some little distance away gave enough light through the **murk** of the rain that was again falling in **torrents** to make it entirely plain that "no

resume[d] *(verb)* to occupy again; to take again

resentful *(adjective)* full of negative feelings
ironically *(adverb)* in an ironic manner
disposed *(adjective)* ready; inclined

needless *(adjective)* useless; not required

one was there." In truth there was nothing but the sheer blank wall of the tower.

Dampier closed the window and signing me to my seat **resumed** his own.

The incident was not in itself particularly mysterious; any one of a dozen explanations was possible (though none has occurred to me), yet it impressed me strangely, the more, perhaps, from my friend's effort to reassure me, which seemed to dignify it with a certain significance and importance. He had proved that no one was there, but in that fact lay all the interest; and he proffered no explanation. His silence was irritating and made me **resentful**.

"My good friend," I said, somewhat **ironically,** I fear, "I am not **disposed** to question your right to harbor as many spooks as you find agreeable to your taste and consistent with your notions of companionship; that is no business of mine. But being just a plain man of affairs, mostly of this world, I find spooks **needless** to my peace and comfort. I am going to my hotel, where my fellow-guests are still in the flesh."

It was not a very civil speech, but he manifested

susurration *(noun)* murmur
boughs *(noun)* branches

occupy[ied] *(verb)* to inhabit

quarter *(noun)* neighborhood
neglect *(noun)* disrepair
primitive *(adjective)* simplistic; naive
suit[ed] *(verb)* to meet the tastes of
maturing *(adjective)* developing

no feeling about it. "Kindly remain," he said. "I am grateful for your presence here. What you have heard to-night I believe myself to have heard twice before. Now I KNOW it was no illusion. That is much to me—more than you know. Have a fresh cigar and a good stock of patience while I tell you the story."

The rain was now falling more steadily, with a low, monotonous **susurration**, interrupted at long intervals by the sudden slashing of the **boughs** of the trees as the wind rose and failed. The night was well advanced, but both sympathy and curiosity held me a willing listener to my friend's monologue, which I did not interrupt by a single word from beginning to end.

"Ten years ago," he said, "I **occupied** a ground-floor apartment in one of a row of houses, all alike, away at the other end of the town, on what we call Rincon Hill. This had been the best **quarter** of San Francisco, but had fallen into **neglect** and decay, partly because the **primitive** character of its domestic architecture no longer **suited** the **maturing** tastes of our wealthy citizens, partly because certain public improvements had made a

bisect[ed] *(verb)* to cut in half

profusely *(adverb)* in an extravagant or abundant manner

beribboned *(adjective)* covered in ribbons

exquisite *(adjective)* beautiful; perfect

matchless *(adjective)* without an equal

move me *(idiom)* causing strong feelings

impropriety *(noun)* something improper or rude

wreck of it. The row of dwellings in one of which I lived stood a little way back from the street, each having a miniature garden, separated from its neighbors by low iron fences and **bisected** with mathematical precision by a box-bordered gravel walk from gate to door.

"One morning as I was leaving my lodging I observed a young girl entering the adjoining garden on the left. It was a warm day in June, and she was lightly gowned in white. From her shoulders hung a broad straw hat **profusely** decorated with flowers and wonderfully **beribboned** in the fashion of the time. My attention was not long held by the **exquisite** simplicity of her costume, for no one could look at her face and think of anything earthly. Do not fear; I shall not profane it by description; it was beautiful exceedingly. All that I had ever seen or dreamed of loveliness was in that **matchless** living picture by the hand of the Divine Artist. So deeply did it **move me** that, without a thought of the **impropriety** of the act, I unconsciously bared my head, as a devout Catholic or well-bred Protestant uncovers before an image of the Blessed Virgin. The maiden

incomparable *(adjective)* unable to be compared; ultimate

penitence *(noun)* remorse; sorrow for sinful actions

poignant *(adjective)* full of emotion

affect[ing] *(verb)* to fake; to pretend

aimlessly *(adverb)* in an unplanned manner

folly *(noun)* bad behavior

showed no displeasure; she merely turned her glorious dark eyes upon me with a look that made me catch my breath, and without other recognition of my act passed into the house. For a moment I stood motionless, hat in hand, painfully conscious of my rudeness, yet so dominated by the emotion inspired by that vision of **incomparable** beauty that my **penitence** was less **poignant** than it should have been. Then I went my way, leaving my heart behind. In the natural course of things I should probably have remained away until nightfall, but by the middle of the afternoon I was back in the little garden, **affecting** an interest in the few foolish flowers that I had never before observed. My hope was vain; she did not appear.

"To a night of unrest succeeded a day of expectation and disappointment, but on the day after, as I wandered **aimlessly** about the neighborhood, I met her. Of course I did not repeat my **folly** of uncovering, nor venture by even so much as too long a look to manifest an interest in her; yet my heart was beating audibly. I trembled and consciously colored as she turned her big black eyes upon me with a look of obvious recognition

devoid *(adjective)* lacking

coquetry *(noun)* flirtatious behavior

particulars *(noun)* details

making [her] acquaintance *(idiom)* to meet

forbearance *(noun)* patience

alliance *(noun)* a beneficial association

condemn *(verb)* to sentence; to doom to a fate

ranks *(noun)* people who are grouped together

deprecate *(verb)* to disapprove of

entirely **devoid** of boldness or **coquetry.**

"I will not weary you with **particulars;** many times afterward I met the maiden, yet never either addressed her or sought to fix her attention. Nor did I take any action toward **making her acquaintance.** Perhaps my **forbearance,** requiring so supreme an effort of self-denial, will not be entirely clear to you. That I was heels over head in love is true, but who can overcome his habit of thought, or reconstruct his character?

"I was what some foolish persons are pleased to call, and others, more foolish, are pleased to be called—an aristocrat; and despite her beauty, her charms and graces, the girl was not of my class. I had learned her name—which it is needless to speak—and something of her family. She was an orphan, a dependent niece of the impossible elderly fat woman in whose lodging-house she lived. My income was small and I lacked the talent for marrying; it is perhaps a gift. An **alliance** with that family would **condemn** me to its manner of life, part me from my books and studies, and in a social sense reduce me to the **ranks.** It is easy to **deprecate** such considerations as these

retain[ed] *(verb)* to employ; to secure

mitigation *(noun)* relief
mandate *(noun)* command; order
heredity *(noun)* inheritance
globule *(noun)* a ball of liquid

irreclaimable *(adjective)* unreformed

vulgarize *(verb)* to make vulgar or coarse

dictate[d] *(verb)* to order; to require

and I have not **retained** myself for the defense. Let judgment be entered against me, but in strict justice all my ancestors for generations should be made co-defendants and I be permitted to plead in **mitigation** of punishment the imperious **mandate** of **heredity**. To a mismatched marriage of that kind every **globule** of my ancestral blood spoke in opposition. In brief, my tastes, habits, instinct, with whatever of reason my love had left me—all fought against it. Moreover, I was an **irreclaimable** sentimentalist, and found a subtle charm in an impersonal and spiritual relation which acquaintance might **vulgarize** and marriage would certainly dispel. No woman, I argued, is what this lovely creature seems. Love is a delicious dream; why should I bring about my own awakening?

"The course **dictated** by all this sense and sentiment was obvious. Honor, pride, prudence, preservation of my ideals—all commanded me to go away, but for that I was too weak. The utmost that I could do by a mighty effort of will was to cease meeting the girl, and that I did. I even avoided the chance encounters of the garden, leaving my

trance *(noun)* a state of being unaware of
   surroundings

traceable *(adjective)* noted; delineated

coarse *(adjective)* vulgar

rebuke *(noun)* criticism

decency *(noun)* propriety; standards
desist *(verb)* to stop

infernal *(adjective)* diabolical; relating to the
   world of the dead
flinging down *(idiom)* throwing down

lodging only when I knew that she had gone to her music lessons, and returning after nightfall. Yet all the while I was as one in a **trance**, indulging the most fascinating fancies and ordering my entire intellectual life in accordance with my dream. Ah, my friend, as one whose actions have a **traceable** relation to reason, you cannot know the fool's paradise in which I lived.

"One evening the devil put it into my head to be an unspeakable idiot. By apparently careless and purposeless questioning I learned from my gossipy landlady that the young woman's bedroom adjoined my own, a party-wall between. Yielding to a sudden and **coarse** impulse I gently rapped on the wall. There was no response, naturally, but I was in no mood to accept a **rebuke**. A madness was upon me and I repeated the folly, the offense, but again ineffectually, and I had the **decency** to **desist**.

"An hour later, while absorbed in some of my **infernal** studies, I heard, or thought I heard, my signal answered. **Flinging down** my books I sprang to the wall and as steadily as my beating heart would permit gave three slow taps upon

elicit *(verb)* to gather information

deliriously *(adverb)* in a disturbed or disorderly manner

perversity *(noun)* impropriety; corruption

persevere[d] *(verb)* to overcome; to persist

timidity *(noun)* the state of being fearful; not brave

haunt[ed] *(verb)* to visit regularly; to frequent

dejection *(noun)* sad or low feelings

unconquerable *(adjective)* not able to be conquered or overcome

it. This time the response was distinct, unmistakable: one, two, three—an exact repetition of my signal. That was all I could **elicit**, but it was enough—too much.

"The next evening, and for many evenings afterward, that folly went on, I always having 'the last word.' During the whole period I was **deliriously** happy, but with the **perversity** of my nature I **persevered** in my resolution not to see her. Then, as I should have expected, I got no further answers. 'She is disgusted,' I said to myself, 'with what she thinks my **timidity** in making no more definite advances'; and I resolved to seek her and make her acquaintance and—what? I did not know, nor do I now know, what might have come of it. I know only that I passed days and days trying to meet her, and all in vain; she was invisible as well as inaudible. I **haunted** the streets where we had met, but she did not come. From my window I watched the garden in front of her house, but she passed neither in nor out. I fell into the deepest **dejection**, believing that she had gone away, yet took no steps to resolve my doubt by inquiry of my landlady, to whom, indeed, I had taken an **unconquerable**

reverence *(noun)* honor or respect
befitting *(adjective)* appropriate
despondency *(noun)* hopelessness

malign *(verb)* to say bad things about; to slander

intervene[d] *(verb)* to become involved

retaliation *(noun)* revenge

fortify[ing] *(verb)* to strengthen; to encourage
obstinacy *(noun)* stubbornness

aversion from her having once spoken of the girl with less of **reverence** than I thought **befitting**.

"There came a fateful night. Worn out with emotion, irresolution and **despondency**, I had retired early and fallen into such sleep as was still possible to me. In the middle of the night something—some **malign** power bent upon the wrecking of my peace forever—caused me to open my eyes and sit up, wide awake and listening intently for I knew not what. Then I thought I heard a faint tapping on the wall—the mere ghost of the familiar signal. In a few moments it was repeated: one, two, three—no louder than before, but addressing a sense alert and strained to receive it. I was about to reply when the Adversary of Peace again **intervened** in my affairs with a rascally suggestion of **retaliation**. She had long and cruelly ignored me; now I would ignore her. Incredible foolishness—may God forgive it! All the rest of the night I lay awake, **fortifying** my **obstinacy** with shameless justifications and—listening.

"Late the next morning, as I was leaving the house, I met my landlady, entering.

"'Good morning, Mr. Dampier,' she said. 'Have

stupor *(noun)* a cloudy mental state; daze
delirium *(noun)* a confused mental state
utterance *(noun)* statement
vagary *(noun)* an unpredictable action
comply[ied] *(verb)* to go along with; to conform
exert[ed] *(verb)* to make an effort

allegiance *(noun)* faithfulness; devotion

you heard the news?'

"I replied in words that I had heard no news; in manner, that I did not care to hear any. The manner escaped her observation.

"'About the sick young lady next door,' she babbled on. 'What! You did not know? Why, she has been ill for weeks. And now—'

"I almost sprang upon her. 'And now,' I cried, 'now what?'

"'She is dead.'

"That is not the whole story. In the middle of the night, as I learned later, the patient, awakening from a long **stupor** after a week of **delirium**, had asked—it was her last **utterance**—that her bed be moved to the opposite side of the room. Those in attendance had thought the request a symptom of her delirium, but had **complied**. And there the poor passing soul had **exerted** its failing will to restore a broken connection—a golden thread of sentiment between its innocence and a monstrous baseness owning a blind, brutal **allegiance** to the Law of Self.

"What reparation could I make? Are there masses that can be said for the repose of souls that are

skeptical *(adjective)* incredulous; disbelieving

hideous *(adjective)* repulsive; offensive
impertinence *(noun)* unsuitable thing; incivility
bid [bade] *(verb)* to tell

abroad such nights as this—spirits 'blown about by the viewless winds'—coming in the storm and darkness with signs and portents, hints of memory and presages of doom?

"This is the third visitation. On the first occasion I was too skeptical to do more than verify by natural methods the character of the incident; on the second, I responded to the signal after it had been several times repeated, but without result. To-night's recurrence completes the 'fatal triad' expounded by Parapelius Necromantius. There is no more to tell."

When Dampier had finished his story I could think of nothing relevant that I cared to say, and to question him would have been a hideous impertinence. I rose and bade him good night in a way to convey to him a sense of my sympathy, which he silently acknowledged by a pressure of the hand. That night, alone with his sorrow and remorse, he passed into the Unknown.

content itself *(idiom)* satisfy itself
afflicted *(adjective)* suffering; tormented
persist[ed] *(verb)* to continue
mortal *(adjective)* hostile; severe

spectral *(adjective)* ghostly

without avail *(idiom)* without success

just the same *(idiom)* no matter what
miasmatic *(adjective)* corrupting

The Water Ghost of Harrowby Hall

by John Kendrick Bangs

The trouble with Harrowby Hall was that it was haunted, and, what was worse, the ghost did not **content itself** with merely appearing at the bedside of the **afflicted** person who saw it, but **persisted** in remaining there for one **mortal** hour before it would disappear.

It never appeared except on Christmas Eve, and then as the clock was striking twelve, in which respect alone was it lacking in that originality which in these days is a sine qua non of success in **spectral** life. The owners of Harrowby Hall had done their utmost to rid themselves of the damp and dewy lady who rose up out of the best bedroom floor at midnight, but **without avail**. They had tried stopping the clock, so that the ghost would not know when it was midnight; but she made her appearance **just the same**, with that fearful **miasmatic** personality of hers, and there

saturated *(adjective)* soaked with water

calk[ed] *(verb)* to close up leaks

unexorcised *(adjective)* the state of not having had evil spirits removed

suffice *(verb)* to meet the needs of

cavernous *(adjective)* large and empty like a cavern

aqueously *(adverb)* very watery or liquid-like in degree

entwined *(adjective)* twisted together

swoon[ed] *(verb)* to faint

she would stand until everything about her was thoroughly **saturated**.

Then the owners of Harrowby Hall **calked** up every crack in the floor with the very best quality of hemp, and over this was placed layers of tar and canvas; the walls were made water-proof, and the doors and windows likewise, the proprietors having conceived the notion that the **unexorcised** lady would find it difficult to leak into the room after these precautions had been taken; but even this did not **suffice**. The following Christmas Eve she appeared as promptly as before, and frightened the occupant of the room quite out of his senses by sitting down alongside of him and gazing with her **cavernous** blue eyes into his; and he noticed, too, that in her long, **aqueously** bony fingers bits of dripping sea-weed were **entwined**, the ends hanging down, and these ends she drew across his forehead until he became like one insane. And then he **swooned** away, and was found unconscious in his bed the next morning by his host, simply saturated with sea-water and fright, from the combined effects of which he never recovered, dying four years later of pneumonia and nervous

prostration *(noun)* collapse

disagreeable *(adjective)* discomforting;
   unpleasant
unavailing *(adjective)* not useful
precede[d] to go before

undiluted *(adjective)* at full strength
felicitate[ing] *(verb)* to congratulate
foil[ed] *(verb)* to prevent; to defeat

prostration at the age of seventy-eight.

The next year the master of Harrowby Hall decided not to have the best spare bedroom opened at all, thinking that perhaps the ghost's thirst for making herself **disagreeable** would be satisfied by haunting the furniture, but the plan was as **unavailing** as the many that had **preceded** it.

The ghost appeared as usual in the room—that is, it was supposed she did, for the hangings were dripping wet the next morning, and in the parlor below the haunted room a great damp spot appeared on the ceiling. Finding no one there, she immediately set out to learn the reason why, and she chose none other to haunt than the owner of the Harrowby himself. She found him in his own cozy room drinking whiskey—whiskey **undiluted**—and **felicitating** himself upon having **foiled** her ghostship, when all of a sudden the curl went out of his hair, his whiskey bottle filled and overflowed, and he was himself in a condition similar to that of a man who has fallen into a water well. When he recovered from the shock, which was a painful one, he saw before

came to *(idiom)* regain consciousness
vast *(adjective)* huge; enormous

fond of *(idiom)* feeling affectionate toward
quenching *(adjective)* extinguishing
daunt[ed] *(verb)* to be subdued
apparition *(noun)* ghost; unexplained
    phenomenon

[hour] was up *(idiom)* was over

duck[ing] *(noun)* to plunge into

him the lady of the cavernous eyes and sea-weed fingers. The sight was so unexpected and so terrifying that he fainted, but immediately **came to**, because of the **vast** amount of water in his hair, which, trickling down over his face, restored his consciousness.

Now it so happened that the master of Harrowby was a brave man, and while he was not particularly **fond of** interviewing ghosts, especially such **quenching** ghosts as the one before him, he was not to be **daunted** by an **apparition**. He had paid the lady the compliment of fainting from the effects of his first surprise, and now that he had come to he intended to find out a few things he felt he had a right to know. He would have liked to put on a dry suit of clothes first, but the apparition declined to leave him for an instant until her **hour was up**, and he was forced to deny himself that pleasure. Every time he would move she would follow him, with the result that everything she came in contact with got a **ducking**. In an effort to warm himself up he approached the fire, an unfortunate move as it turned out, because it brought the ghost directly over the fire,

extinguish[ed] *(verb)* to put out; to stop burning

ward off *(idiom)* to keep away

interfere *(verb)* to get in the way; to intrude

asperity *(noun)* roughness; harshness

far be it from me *(idiom)* to explain why it is not something typically done

infernal *(adjective)* diabolical; relating to the world of the dead

implore *(verb)* to beg; to beseech

gurgling *(adjective)* sounding like water

which immediately was **extinguished**. The whiskey became utterly valueless as a comforter to his chilled system, because it was by this time diluted to a proportion of ninety percent of water. The only thing he could do to **ward off** the evil effects of his encounter he did, and that was to swallow ten two-grain quinine pills, which he managed to put into his mouth before the ghost had time to **interfere**. Having done this, he turned with some **asperity** to the ghost, and said:

"**Far be it from me** to be impolite to a woman, madam, but I'm hanged if it wouldn't please me better if you'd stop these **infernal** visits of yours to this house. Go sit out on the lake, if you like that sort of thing; soak the water-butt, if you wish; but do not, I **implore** you, come into a gentleman's house and saturate him and his possessions in this way. It is very disagreeable."

"Henry Hartwick Oglethorpe," said the ghost, in a **gurgling** voice, "you don't know what you are talking about."

"Madam," returned the unhappy householder, "I wish that remark were strictly truthful. I was talking about you. It would be shillings and

specious *(adjective)* false; deceptive

indignation *(noun)* anger; rage

irrelevant *(adjective)* not applicable to anything else

impertinence *(noun)* unsuitable thing; incivility

compelled to *(idiom)* urged to

inexorable *(adjective)* unstoppable; relentless

aspire[d] *(verb)* to hope to accomplish

incumbent *(noun)* occupant; holder of a position

pence—nay, pounds, in my pocket, madam, if I did not know you."

"That is a bit of **specious** nonsense," returned the ghost, throwing a quart of **indignation** into the face of the master of Harrowby. "It may rank high as repartee, but as a comment upon my statement that you do not know what you are talking about, it savors of **irrelevant impertinence**. You do not know that I am **compelled to** haunt this place year after year by **inexorable** fate. It is no pleasure to me to enter this house, and ruin and mildew everything I touch. I never **aspired** to be a shower-bath, but it is my doom. Do you know who I am?"

"No, I don't," returned the master of Harrowby. "I should say you were the Lady of the Lake, or Little Sallie Waters."

"You are a witty man for your years," said the ghost.

"Well, my humor is drier than yours ever will be," returned the master.

"No doubt. I'm never dry. I am the Water Ghost of Harrowby Hall, and dryness is a quality entirely beyond my wildest hope. I have been the **incumbent** of this highly unpleasant office for

specter *(noun)* ghost

induce[d] *(verb)* to persuade; to cause to do
    something
predicament *(noun)* an uncomfortable situation

deem *(verb)* to think; to consider

two hundred years to-night."

"How in the world did you ever come to get elected?" asked the master.

"Through a suicide," replied the **specter**. "I am the ghost of that fair maiden whose picture hangs over the mantel-piece in the drawing-room. I should have been your great-great-great-great-great-aunt if I had lived, Henry Hartwick Oglethorpe, for I was the own sister of your great-great-great-great-grandfather."

"But what **induced** you to get this house into such a **predicament**?"

"I was not to blame, sir," returned the lady. "It was my father's fault. He it was who built Harrowby Hall, and the haunted chamber was to have been mine. My father had it furnished in pink and yellow, knowing well that blue and gray formed the only combination of color I could tolerate. He did it merely to spite me, and, with what I **deem** a proper spirit, I declined to live in the room; whereupon my father said I could live there or on the lawn, he didn't care which. That night I ran from the house and jumped over the cliff into the sea."

rash *(adjective)* hasty

consequence[s] *(noun)* the result of an action

inhabited *(adjective)* occupied; lived in

allotted *(adjective)* assigned

divulge *(verb)* to tell; to reveal

"That was **rash**," said the master of Harrowby.

"So I've heard," returned the ghost. "If I had known what the **consequences** were to be I should not have jumped; but I really never realized what I was doing until after I was drowned. I had been drowned a week when a sea-nymph came to me and informed me that I was to be one of her followers forever afterwards, adding that it should be my doom to haunt Harrowby Hall for one hour every Christmas Eve throughout the rest of eternity. I was to haunt that room on such Christmas Eves as I found it **inhabited**; and if it should turn out not to be inhabited, I was and am to spend the **allotted** hour with the head of the house."

"I'll sell the place."

"That you cannot do, for it is also required of me that I shall appear as the deeds are to be delivered to any purchaser, and **divulge** to him the awful secret of the house."

"Do you mean to tell me that on every Christmas Eve that I don't happen to have somebody in that guest-chamber, you are going to haunt me wherever I may be, ruining my whiskey, taking all the curl out of my hair, extinguishing my fire, and

douse *(verb)* to soak with water; to drench

trickle *(noun)* a small amount of something moving slowly

ejaculate[d] to say suddenly

wager *(noun)* bet; stake

soaking me through to the skin?" demanded the master.

"You have stated the case, Oglethorpe. And what is more," said the water ghost, "it doesn't make the slightest difference where you are, if I find that room empty, wherever you may be I shall **douse** you with my spectral pres—"

Here the clock struck one, and immediately the apparition faded away. It was perhaps more of a **trickle** than a fade, but as a disappearance it was complete.

"By St. George and his Dragon!" **ejaculated** the master of Harrowby, wringing his hands. "It is guineas to hot-cross buns that next Christmas there's an occupant of the spare room, or I spend the night in a bath-tub."

But the master of Harrowby would have lost his **wager** had there been any one there to take him up, for when Christmas Eve came again he was in his grave, never having recovered from the cold contracted that awful night. Harrowby Hall was closed, and the heir to the estate was in London, where to him in his chambers came the same experience that his father had gone

onslaught *(noun)* attack

drenched *(adjective)* soaked with water

vacate *(verb)* to leave; to give up

inflict[ed] *(verb)* to cause someone to suffer

mystic *(adjective)* magical; mysterious
weary *(adjective)* tired

aught *(noun)* nothing

through, saving only that, being younger and stronger, he survived the shock. Everything in his rooms was ruined—his clocks were rusted in the works; a fine collection of water-color drawings was entirely obliterated by the **onslaught** of the water ghost; and what was worse, the apartments below his were **drenched** with the water soaking through the floors, a damage for which he was compelled to pay, and which resulted in his being requested by his landlady to **vacate** the premises immediately.

The story of the visitation **inflicted** upon his family had gone abroad, and no one could be got to invite him out to any function save afternoon teas and receptions. Fathers of daughters declined to permit him to remain in their houses later than eight o'clock at night, not knowing but that some emergency might arise in the supernatural world which would require the unexpected appearance of the water ghost in this on nights other than Christmas Eve, and before the **mystic** hour when **weary** churchyards, ignoring the rules which are supposed to govern polite society, begin to yawn. Nor would the maids themselves have **aught** to do

incursion *(noun)* raid; violent entrance into

crucial *(adjective)* critical; important

consent *(noun)* permission; approval

ingenuity *(noun)* cleverness

with him, fearing the destruction by the sudden **incursion** of aqueous femininity of the costumes which they held most dear.

So the heir of Harrowby Hall resolved, as his ancestors for several generations before him had resolved, that something must be done. His first thought was to make one of his servants occupy the haunted room at the **crucial** moment; but in this he failed, because the servants themselves knew the history of that room and rebelled. None of his friends would **consent** to sacrifice their personal comfort to his, nor was there to be found in all England a man so poor as to be willing to occupy the doomed chamber on Christmas Eve for pay.

Then the thought came to the heir to have the fireplace in the room enlarged, so that he might evaporate the ghost at its first appearance, and he was felicitating himself upon the **ingenuity** of his plan, when he remembered what his father had told him—how that no fire could withstand the lady's extremely contagious dampness. And then he thought of the steam-pipes. These, he remembered, could lie hundreds of feet deep in water, and still retain sufficient heat to drive the water

withering *(adjective)* devastating

outlay *(noun)* payment; expenditure
remedy *(verb)* to cure; to correct

avail *(verb)* to result in

rehabilitated *(adjective)* restored
exasperatingly *(adverb)* in a frustrating manner

away in vapor; and as a result of this thought the haunted room was heated by steam to a **withering** degree, and the heir for six months attended daily the Turkish baths, so that when Christmas Eve came he could himself withstand the awful temperature of the room.

The scheme was only partially successful. The water ghost appeared at the specified time, and found the heir of Harrowby prepared; but hot as the room was, it shortened her visit by no more than five minutes in the hour, during which time the nervous system of the young master was nearly shattered, and the room itself was cracked and warped to an extent which required the **outlay** of a large sum of money to **remedy**. And worse than this, as the last drop of the water ghost was slowly sizzling itself out on the floor, she whispered to her would-be conqueror that his scheme would **avail** him nothing, because there was still water in great plenty where she came from, and that next year would find her **rehabilitated** and as **exasperatingly** saturating as ever.

It was then that the natural action of the mind, in going from one extreme to the other, suggested

bitterly *(adverb)* in an angry manner

campaign against *(idiom)*

clad *(adjective)* dressed

to the ingenious heir of Harrowby the means by which the water ghost was ultimately conquered, and happiness once more came within the grasp of the house of Oglethorpe.

The heir provided himself with a warm suit of fur under-clothing. Donning this with the furry side in, he placed over it a rubber garment, tight-fitting, which he wore just as a woman wears a jersey. On top of this he placed another set of under-clothing, this suit made of wool, and over this was a second rubber garment like the first. Upon his head he placed a light and comfortable diving helmet, and so clad, on the following Christmas Eve he awaited the coming of his tormentor.

It was a **bitterly** cold night that brought to a close this twenty-fourth day of December. The air outside was still, but the temperature was below zero. Within all was quiet, the servants of Harrowby Hall awaiting with beating hearts the outcome of their master's **campaign against** his supernatural visitor.

The master himself was lying on the bed in the haunted room, **clad** as has already been indicated, and then—

clanged out *(idiom)* rang

heir *(noun)* someone who inherits money or is
  entitled to something
rivulets *(noun)* a stream

courteously *(adverb)* politely

delectable *(adjective)* delightful; pleasant

The clock **clanged out** the hour of twelve.

There was a sudden banging of doors, a blast of cold air swept through the halls, the door leading into the haunted chamber flew open, a splash was heard, and the water ghost was seen standing at the side of the **heir** of Harrowby, from whose outer dress there streamed **rivulets** of water, but whose own person deep down under the various garments he wore was as dry and as warm as he could have wished.

"Ha!" said the young master of Harrowby. "I'm glad to see you."

"You are the most original man I've met, if that is true," returned the ghost. "May I ask where did you get that hat?"

"Certainly, madam," returned the master, **courteously.** "It is a little portable observatory I had made for just such emergencies as this. But, tell me, is it true that you are doomed to follow me about for one mortal hour—to stand where I stand, to sit where I sit?"

"That is my **delectable** fate," returned the lady.

"We'll go out on the lake," said the master, starting up.

reluctance *(noun)* disinclination; unwillingness

ripple *(verb)* to move like a wave

distress *(noun)* trouble; suffering

beseech *(verb)* to beg; to implore
oblige *(verb)* to do a favor

"You can't get rid of me that way," returned the ghost. "The water won't swallow me up; in fact, it will just add to my present bulk."

"Nevertheless," said the master, firmly, "we will go out on the lake."

"But, my dear sir," returned the ghost, with a pale reluctance, "it is fearfully cold out there. You will be frozen hard before you've been out ten minutes."

"Oh no, I'll not," replied the master. "I am very warmly dressed. Come!" This last in a tone of command that made the ghost ripple.

And they started.

They had not gone far before the water ghost showed signs of distress.

"You walk too slowly," she said. "I am nearly frozen. My knees are so stiff now I can hardly move. I beseech you to accelerate your step."

"I should like to oblige a lady," returned the master, courteously, "but my clothes are rather heavy, and a hundred yards an hour is about my speed. Indeed, I think we would better sit down here on this snowdrift, and talk matters over."

"Do not! Do not do so, I beg!" cried the ghost.

rigid *(adjective)* stiff; inflexible

fetters *(noun)* restraints

congeal *(verb)* to make stiff or rigid

tepid *(adjective)* unenthusiastic; dispassionate

"Let me move on. I feel myself growing **rigid** as it is. If we stop here, I shall be frozen stiff."

"That, madam," said the master slowly, and seating himself on an ice-cake—"that is why I have brought you here. We have been on this spot just ten minutes, we have fifty more. Take your time about it, madam, but freeze, that is all I ask of you."

"I cannot move my right leg now," cried the ghost, in despair, "and my overskirt is a solid sheet of ice. Oh, good, kind Mr. Oglethorpe, light a fire, and let me go free from these icy **fetters**."

"Never, madam. It cannot be. I have you at last."

"Alas!" cried the ghost, a tear trickling down her frozen cheek. "Help me, I beg. I **congeal**!"

"Congeal, madam, congeal!" returned Oglethorpe, coldly. "You have drenched me and mine for two hundred and three years, madam. To-night you have had your last drench."

"Ah, but I shall thaw out again, and then you'll see. Instead of the comfortably **tepid**, genial ghost I have been in my past, sir, I shall be iced-water," cried the lady, threateningly.

"No, you won't, either," returned Oglethorpe;

asbestos *(noun)* a fibrous, fire-proof material

ill-suppressed *(adjective)* hardly subdued
chuckle *(noun)* laugh

momentary *(adjective)* lasting only a moment;
    fleeting
tremor *(noun)* slight movement; trembling

"for when you are frozen quite stiff, I shall send you to a cold-storage warehouse, and there shall you remain an icy work of art forever more."

"But warehouses burn."

"So they do, but this warehouse cannot burn. It is made of **asbestos** and surrounding it are fire-proof walls, and within those walls the temperature is now and shall forever be 416 degrees below the zero point; low enough to make an icicle of any flame in this world—or the next," the master added, with an **ill-suppressed chuckle.**

"For the last time let me beseech you. I would go on my knees to you, Oglethorpe, were they not already frozen. I beg of you do not doo—"

Here even the words froze on the water ghost's lips and the clock struck one. There was a **momentary tremor** throughout the ice-bound form, and the moon, coming out from behind a cloud, shone down on the rigid figure of a beautiful woman sculptured in clear, transparent ice. There stood the ghost of Harrowby Hall, conquered by the cold, a prisoner for all time.

The heir of Harrowby had won at last, and to-day in a large storage house in London stands the

woe *(noun)* sadness; grief
cope[ing] *(verb)* to deal with stress

linger[s] *(verb)* to remain in existence
far from being *(idiom)* implying the opposite of
whatever is stated

[before the year] is out *(idiom)* is over

frigid form of one who will never again flood the house of Oglethorpe with **woe** and sea-water.

As for the heir of Harrowby, his success in **coping** with a ghost has made him famous, a fame that still **lingers** about him, although his victory took place some twenty years ago; and so **far from being** unpopular with the fair sex, as he was when we first knew him, he has not only been married twice, but is to lead a third bride to the altar **before the year is out.**

vantage-point *(noun)* point of view

scarcely *(adverb)* hardly

frenzied *(adjective)* wild; agitated

shudder *(verb)* to shake; to shiver

wont *(noun)* habit
untenanted *(adjective)* unlived in; uninhabited

Luella Miller

by Mary Wilkins Freeman

Close to the village street stood the one-story
house in which Luella Miller, who had an evil
name in the village, had dwelt. She had been dead
for years, yet there were those in the village who, in
spite of the clearer light which comes on a **vantage-
point** from a long-past danger, half believed in
the tale which they had heard from their child-
hood. In their hearts, although they **scarcely**
would have owned it, was a survival of the wild
horror and **frenzied** fear of their ancestors who
had dwelt in the same age with Luella Miller.
Young people even would stare with a **shudder** at
the old house as they passed, and children never
played around it as was their **wont** around an
untenanted building. Not a window in the old
Miller house was broken: the panes reflected the
morning sunlight in patches of emerald and blue,
and the latch of the sagging front door was never

kindred *(noun)* family relatives

score *(noun)* twenty

dark *(adjective)* evil
testify[ied] *(verb)* to tell; to make a statement
exalted *(adjective)* high; elevated

fallen a victim *(idiom)* to become a victim

vagrant *(noun)* wanderer; nomad
unhallowed *(adjective)* unholy; not revered
superstitious *(adjective)* fearing beliefs that cannot be proved

lifted, although no bolt secured it. Since Luella Miller had been carried out of it, the house had had no tenant except one friendless old soul who had no choice between that and the far-off shelter of the open sky. This old woman, who had survived her **kindred** and friends, lived in the house one week, then one morning no smoke came out of the chimney, and a body of neighbors, a **score** strong, entered and found her dead in her bed. There were **dark** whispers as to the cause of her death, and there were those who **testified** to an expression of fear so **exalted** that it showed forth the state of the departing soul upon the dead face. The old woman had been hale and hearty when she entered the house, and in seven days she was dead; it seemed that she had **fallen a victim** to some uncanny power. The minister talked in the pulpit with covert severity against the sin of superstition; still the belief prevailed. Not a soul in the village but would have chosen the almshouse rather than that dwelling. No **vagrant**, if he heard the tale, would seek shelter beneath that old roof, **unhallowed** by nearly half a century of **superstitious** fear.

marvel *(noun)* a wonder; an astonishment

vitality *(noun)* physical and mental force

garrulousness *(noun)* the state of being overly talkative

essay[ed] *(verb)* to attempt; to try

wittingly *(adverb)* in an intentional manner

vernacular *(noun)* dialect; language

slight *(adjective)* slim; frail

pliant *(adjective)* readily influenced; yielding

There was only one person in the village who had actually known Luella Miller. That person was a woman well over eighty, but a **marvel** of **vitality** and unextinct youth. Straight as an arrow, with the spring of one recently let loose from the bow of life, she moved about the streets, and she always went to church, rain or shine. She had never married, and had lived alone for years in a house across the road from Luella Miller's.

This woman had none of the **garrulousness** of age, but never in all her life had she ever held her tongue for any will save her own, and she never spared the truth when she **essayed** to present it. She it was who bore testimony to the life, evil, though possibly **wittingly** or designedly so, of Luella Miller, and to her personal appearance. When this old woman spoke—and she had the gift of description, although her thoughts were clothed in the rude **vernacular** of her native village—one could seem to see Luella Miller as she had really looked. According to this woman, Lydia Anderson by name, Luella Miller had been a beauty of a type rather unusual in New England. She had been a **slight**, **pliant** sort of creature,

fair *(adjective)* light colored

pleading *(noun)* asking; entreating

was a sight to see *(idiom)* it was remarkable

a sight of *(idiom)* a lot of; many

handsome *(adjective)* beautiful; physically
    appealing

as ready with a strong yielding to fate and as unbreakable as a willow. She had glimmering lengths of straight, **fair** hair, which she wore softly looped round a long, lovely face. She had blue eyes full of soft **pleading**, little slender, clinging hands, and a wonderful grace of motion and attitude.

"Luella Miller used to sit in a way nobody else could if they sat up and studied a week of Sundays," said Lydia Anderson, "and it **was a sight to see** her walk. If one of them willows over there on the edge of the brook could start up and get its roots free of the ground, and move off, it would go just the way Luella Miller used to. She had a green shot silk she used to wear, too, and a hat with green ribbon streamers, and a lace veil blowing across her face and out sideways, and a green ribbon flyin' from her waist. That was what she came out bride in when she married Erastus Miller. Her name before she was married was Hill. There was always **a sight of** "l's" in her name, married or single. Erastus Miller was good lookin', too, better lookin' than Luella. Sometimes I used to think that Luella wa'n't so **handsome** after all. Erastus just about worshiped her. I used to know

splendid *(adjective)* great; superb

ail[ed] *(verb)* to cause discomfort or pain

winked at it *(idiom)* ignored it

fit *(adjective)* suitable; acceptable

him pretty well. He lived next door to me, and we went to school together. Folks used to say he was waitin' on me, but he wa'n't. I never thought he was except once or twice when he said things that some girls might have suspected meant somethin'. That was before Luella came here to teach the district school. It was funny how she came to get it, for folks said she hadn't any education, and that one of the big girls, Lottie Henderson, used to do all the teachin' for her, while she sat back and did embroidery work on a cambric pocket-handkerchief. Lottie Henderson was a real smart girl, a **splendid** scholar, and she just set her eyes by Luella, as all the girls did. Lottie would have made a real smart woman, but she died when Luella had been here about a year—just faded away and died: nobody knew what **ailed** her. She dragged herself to that schoolhouse and helped Luella teach till the very last minute. The committee all knew how Luella didn't do much of the work herself, but they **winked at it.** It wa'n't long after Lottie died that Erastus married her. I always thought he hurried it up because she wa'n't **fit** to teach. One of the big boys used to help her after Lottie

government *(noun)* discretion; good behavior

shut their eyes to things *(idiom)* hardly
acknowledged

consumption *(noun)* tuberculosis

feeble *(adjective)* weak

hunched up *(adjective)* curled up

died, but he hadn't much **government**, and the
school didn't do very well, and Luella might have
had to give it up, for the committee couldn't have
shut their eyes to things much longer. The boy
that helped her was a real honest, innocent sort
of fellow, and he was a good scholar, too. Folks
said he overstudied, and that was the reason he
was took crazy the year after Luella married, but I
don't know. And I don't know what made Erastus
Miller go into **consumption** of the blood the year
after he was married: consumption wa'n't in his
family. He just grew weaker and weaker, and
went almost bent double when he tried to wait on
Luella, and he spoke **feeble**, like an old man. He
worked terrible hard till the last trying to save up
a little to leave Luella. I've seen him out in the
worst storms on a wood-sled—he used to cut and
sell wood—and he was **hunched up** on top lookin'
more dead than alive. Once I couldn't stand it: I
went over and helped him pitch some wood on the
cart—I was always strong in my arms. I wouldn't
stop for all he told me to, and I guess he was glad
enough for the help. That was only a week before
he died. He fell on the kitchen floor while he was

lift her finger *(idiom)* make even the slightest effort

particular *(adjective)* difficult to please; exacting

mite *(noun)* a little

gettin' breakfast. He always got the breakfast and let Luella lay abed. He did all the sweepin' and the washin' and the ironin' and most of the cookin'. He couldn't bear to have Luella **lift her finger**, and she let him do for her. She lived like a queen for all the work she did. She didn't even do her sewin'. She said it made her shoulder ache to sew, and poor Erastus's sister Lily used to do all her sewin'. She wa'n't able to, either; she was never strong in her back, but she did it beautifully. She had to, to suit Luella, she was so dreadful **particular**. I never saw anythin' like the sewing that Lily Miller did for Luella. She made all Luella's weddin' outfit, and that green silk dress, after Maria Babbit cut it. Maria she cut it for nothin', and she did a lot more cuttin' and fittin' for nothin' for Luella, too. Lily Miller went to live with Luella after Erastus died. She gave up her home, though she was real attached to it and wa'n't a **mite** afraid to stay alone. She rented it and she went to live with Luella right away after the funeral."

Then this old woman, Lydia Anderson, who remembered Luella Miller, would go on to relate the story of Lily Miller. It seemed that on the

robust *(adjective)* sturdy; healthy
blooming *(adjective)* glowing with youth and
   beauty
candid *(adjective)* white

wan *(adjective)* sickly; feeble
hollows *(noun)* holes; empty spaces

anxiety *(noun)* fear; concern

removal of Lily Miller to the house of her dead brother, to live with his widow, the village people first began to talk. This Lily Miller had been hardly past her first youth, and a most **robust** and **blooming** woman, rosy-cheeked, with curls of strong, black hair overshadowing round, **candid** temples and bright dark eyes. It was not six months after she had taken up her residence with her sister-in-law that her rosy color faded and her pretty curves became **wan hollows**. White shadows began to show in the black rings of her hair, and the light died out of her eyes, her features sharpened, and there were pathetic lines at her mouth, which yet wore always an expression of utter sweetness and even happiness. She was devoted to her sister; there was no doubt that she loved her with her whole heart, and was perfectly content in her service. It was her sole **anxiety** lest she should die and leave her alone.

"The way Lily Miller used to talk about Luella was enough to make you mad and enough to make you cry," said Lydia Anderson. "I've been in there sometimes toward the last when she was too feeble to cook and carried her some blanc-mange

relish *(verb)* to enjoy

fond of *(idiom)* feeling affectionate toward
pined away *(idiom)* wasted away in longing

droop *(verb)* to become weak

or custard—somethin' I thought she might **relish**, and she'd thank me, and when I asked her how she was, say she felt better than she did yesterday, and asked me if I didn't think she looked better, dreadful pitiful, and say poor Luella had an awful time takin' care of her and doin' the work—she wa'n't strong enough to do anythin'—when all the time Luella wa'n't liftin' her finger and poor Lily didn't get any care except what the neighbors gave her, and Luella eat up everythin' that was carried in for Lily. I had it real straight that she did. Luella used to just sit and cry and do nothin'. She did act real **fond of** Lily, and she **pined away** considerable, too. There was those that thought she'd go into a decline herself. But after Lily died, her Aunt Abby Mixter came, and then Luella picked up and grew as fat and rosy as ever. But poor Aunt Abby begun to **droop** just the way Lily had, and I guess somebody wrote to her married daughter, Mrs. Sam Abbot, who lived in Barre, for she wrote her mother that she must leave right away and come and make her a visit, but Aunt Abby wouldn't go. I can see her now. She was a real good-lookin' woman, tall and large, with a

benevolent *(adjective)* suggesting goodwill or
good feelings

spoke her mind *(idiom)* voice opinions

big, square face and a high forehead that looked
of itself kind of **benevolent** and good. She just
tended out on Luella as if she had been a baby,
and when her married daughter sent for her she
wouldn't stir one inch. She'd always thought a lot
of her daughter, too, but she said Luella needed
her and her married daughter didn't. Her daughter kept writin' and writin', but it didn't do any
good. Finally she came, and when she saw how
bad her mother looked, she broke down and cried
and all but went on her knees to have her come
away. She **spoke her mind** out to Luella, too. She
told her that she'd killed her husband and everybody that had anythin' to do with her, and she'd
thank her to leave her mother alone. Luella went
into hysterics, and Aunt Abby was so frightened
that she called me after her daughter went. Mrs.
Sam Abbot she went away fairly cryin' out loud in
the buggy, the neighbors heard her, and well she
might, for she never saw her mother again alive. I
went in that night when Aunt Abby called for me,
standin' in the door with her little green-checked
shawl over her head. I can see her now. 'Do come
over here, Miss Anderson,' she sung out, kind of

hush *(verb)* to quiet someone

contrive[d] *(verb)* to manage; to succeed but
with difficulty

gasping for breath. I didn't stop for anythin'. I put over as fast as I could, and when I got there, there was Luella laughin' and cryin' all together, and Aunt Abby trying to **hush** her, and all the time she herself was white as a sheet and shakin' so she could hardly stand. 'For the land sakes, Mrs. Mixter,' says I, 'you look worse than she does. You ain't fit to be up out of your bed.'

"'Oh, there ain't anythin' the matter with me,' says she. Then she went on talkin' to Luella. 'There, there, don't, don't, poor little lamb,' says she. 'Aunt Abby is here. She ain't goin' away and leave you. Don't, poor little lamb.'

"'Do leave her with me, Mrs. Mixter, and you get back to bed,' says I, for Aunt Abby had been layin' down considerable lately, though somehow she **contrived** to do the work.

"'I'm well enough,' says she. 'Don't you think she had better have the doctor, Miss Anderson?'

"'The doctor,' says I, 'I think YOU had better have the doctor. I think you need him much worse than some folks I could mention.' And I looked right straight at Luella Miller laughin' and cryin' and goin' on as if she was the center of all creation.

tottery *(noun)* swaying
camphor *(noun)* an aromatic medicine

holler[ed] *(verb)* to yell

All the time she was actin' so—seemed as if she was too sick to sense anythin'—she was keepin' a sharp lookout as to how we took it out of the corner of one eye. I see her. You could never cheat me about Luella Miller. Finally I got real mad and I run home and I got a bottle of sedatives I had, and I poured some boilin' hot water on a handful of catnip, and I mixed up that catnip tea with most half a wineglass of sedative, and I went with it over to Luella's. I marched right up to Luella, a-holdin' out of that cup, all smokin'. 'Now,' says I, 'Luella Miller, YOU SWALLOW THIS!'

"'What is—what is it, oh, what is it?' she sort of screeches out. Then she goes off a-laughin' enough to kill.

"'Poor lamb, poor little lamb,' says Aunt Abby, standin' over her, all kind of **tottery**, and tryin' to bathe her head with **camphor**.

"'YOU SWALLOW THIS RIGHT DOWN,' says I. And I didn't waste any ceremony. I just took hold of Luella Miller's chin and I tipped her head back, and I caught her mouth open with laughin', and I clapped that cup to her lips, and I fairly **hollered** at her: 'Swallow, swallow, swallow!' and she

gulp[ed] *(verb)* to swallow vigorously

sleep like a baby *(idiom)* to sleep deeply and
    peacefully
inside of [half an hour] *(idiom)* in less than

used up *(idiom)* spent; exhausted

gulped it right down. She had to, and I guess it did her good. Anyhow, she stopped cryin' and laughin' and let me put her to bed, and she went to **sleep like a baby inside of half an hour.** That was more than poor Aunt Abby did. She lay awake all that night and I stayed with her, though she tried not to have me; said she wa'n't sick enough for watchers. But I stayed, and I made some good cornmeal gruel and I fed her a teaspoon every little while all night long. It seemed to me as if she was jest dyin' from bein' all wore out. In the mornin' as soon as it was light I run over to the Bisbees and sent Johnny Bisbee for the doctor. I told him to tell the doctor to hurry, and he come pretty quick. Poor Aunt Abby didn't seem to know much of anythin' when he got there. You couldn't hardly tell she breathed, she was so **used up.** When the doctor had gone, Luella came into the room lookin' like a baby in her ruffled nightgown. I can see her now. Her eyes were as blue and her face all pink and white like a blossom, and she looked at Aunt Abby in the bed sort of innocent and surprised. 'Why,' says she, 'Aunt Abby ain't got up yet?'

"'No, she ain't,' says I, pretty short.

dreadful *(adjective)* extremely
astonished *(adjective)* surprised

harm *(noun)* injury; damage

aggrieved *(adjective)* distressed
injured *(adjective)* hurt; harmed

"'I thought I didn't smell the coffee,' says Luella.

"'Coffee,' says I. 'I guess if you have coffee this mornin' you'll make it yourself.'

"'I never made the coffee in all my life,' says she, **dreadful astonished**. 'Erastus always made the coffee as long as he lived, and then Lily she made it, and then Aunt Abby made it. I don't believe I CAN make the coffee, Miss Anderson.'

"'You can make it or go without, jest as you please,' says I.

"'Ain't Aunt Abby goin' to get up?' says she.

"'I guess she won't get up,' says I, 'sick as she is.' I was gettin' madder and madder. There was somethin' about that little pink-and-white thing standin' there and talkin' about coffee, when she had killed so many better folks than she was, and had jest killed another, that made me feel 'most as if I wished somebody would up and kill her before she had a chance to do any more **harm**.

"'Is Aunt Abby sick?' says Luella, as if she was sort of **aggrieved** and **injured**.

"'Yes,' says I, 'she's sick, and she's goin' to die, and then you'll be left alone, and you'll have to do for yourself and wait on yourself, or do without

hard *(adjective)* strict and unfeeling

mind[ed] *(verb)* to pay attention

coddle *(verb)* to care for too attentively; to pamper

low *(adjective)* depressed; weak

nourishment *(noun)* food

things.' I don't know but I was sort of **hard**, but it was the truth, and if I was any harder than Luella Miller had been I'll give up. I ain't never been sorry that I said it. Well, Luella, she up and had hysterics again at that, and I jest let her have 'em. All I did was to bundle her into the room on the other side of the entry where Aunt Abby couldn't hear her, if she wa'n't past it—I don't know but she was—and set her down hard in a chair and told her not to come back into the other room, and she **minded**. She had her hysterics in there till she got tired. When she found out that nobody was comin' to **coddle** her and do for her she stopped. At least I suppose she did. I had all I could do with poor Aunt Abby tryin' to keep the breath of life in her. The doctor had told me that she was dreadful **low**, and give me some very strong medicine to give to her in drops real often, and told me real particular about the **nourishment**. Well, I did as he told me real faithful till she wa'n't able to swallow any longer. Then I had her daughter sent for. I had begun to realize that she wouldn't last any time at all. I hadn't realized it before, though I spoke to Luella the way I did. The doctor he came, and

sharp *(adjective)* quickly; brusquely

severe *(adjective)* harsh; stern
agitate[ing] *(verb)* to disturb; to excite

hysterics *(noun)* unstoppable emotions such as crying or laughing

Mrs. Sam Abbot, but when she got there it was too late; her mother was dead. Aunt Abby's daughter just give one look at her mother layin' there, then she turned sort of **sharp** and sudden and looked at me.

"'Where is she?' says she, and I knew she meant Luella.

"'She's out in the kitchen,' says I. 'She's too nervous to see folks die. She's afraid it will make her sick.'

"The Doctor he speaks up then. He was a young man. Old Doctor Park had died the year before, and this was a young fellow just out of college. 'Mrs. Miller is not strong,' says he, kind of **severe**, 'and she is quite right in not **agitating** herself.'

"'You are another, young man; she's got her pretty claw on you,' thinks I, but I didn't say anythin' to him. I just said over to Mrs. Sam Abbot that Luella was in the kitchen, and Mrs. Sam Abbot she went out there, and I went, too, and I never heard anythin' like the way she talked to Luella Miller. I felt pretty hard to Luella myself, but this was more than I ever would have dared to say. Luella she was too scared to go into **hysterics**.

[fainted] dead away *(idiom)* to lose consciousness as if dead

stream[ing] *(verb)* to extend to full length

She jest flopped. She seemed to jest shrink away to nothin' in that kitchen chair, with Mrs. Sam Abbot standin' over her and talkin' and tellin' her the truth. I guess the truth was most too much for her and no mistake, because Luella presently actually did faint away, and there wa'n't any sham about it, the way I always suspected there was about them hysterics. She **fainted dead away** and we had to lay her flat on the floor, and the Doctor he came runnin' out and he said somethin' about a weak heart dreadful fierce to Mrs. Sam Abbot, but she wa'n't a mite scared. She faced him jest as white as even Luella was layin' there lookin' like death and the Doctor feelin' of her pulse.

"'Weak heart,' says she, 'weak heart; weak fiddle-sticks! There ain't nothin' weak about that woman. She's got strength enough to hang onto other folks till she kills 'em. Weak? It was my poor mother that was weak: this woman killed her as sure as if she had taken a knife to her.'

"But the Doctor he didn't pay much attention. He was bendin' over Luella layin' there with her yellow hair all **streamin'** and her pretty pink-and-white face all pale, and her blue eyes like stars

draw *(verb)* to pull; to lead

gone out, and he was holdin' onto her hand and smoothin' her forehead, and tellin' me to get the brandy in Aunt Abby's room, and I was sure as I wanted to be that Luella had got somebody else to hang onto, now Aunt Abby was gone, and I thought of poor Erastus Miller, and I sort of pitied the poor young Doctor, led away by a pretty face, and I made up my mind I'd see what I could do.

"I waited till Aunt Abby had been dead and buried about a month, and the Doctor was goin' to see Luella steady and folks were beginnin' to talk; then one evenin', when I knew the Doctor had been called out of town and wouldn't be round, I went over to Luella's. I found her all dressed up in a blue muslin with white polka dots on it, and her hair curled jest as pretty, and there wa'n't a young girl in the place could compare with her. There was somethin' about Luella Miller seemed to **draw** the heart right out of you, but she didn't draw it out of ME. She was settin' rocking in the chair by her sittin'-room window, and Maria Brown had gone home. Maria Brown had been in to help her, or rather to do the work, for Luella wa'n't helped when she didn't do anythin'. Maria

capable *(adjective)* able and efficient
ties *(noun)* relatives; relationships

delicate *(adjective)* weak; fragile

bitter *(adjective)* severe

Brown was real **capable** and she didn't have any **ties**; she wa'n't married, and lived alone, so she'd offered. I couldn't see why she should do the work any more than Luella; she wa'n't any too strong; but she seemed to think she could and Luella seemed to think so, too, so she went over and did all the work—washed, and ironed, and baked, while Luella sat and rocked. Maria didn't live long afterward. She began to fade away just the same fashion the others had. Well, she was warned, but she acted real mad when folks said anythin': said Luella was a poor, abused woman, too **delicate** to help herself, and they'd ought to be ashamed, and if she died helpin' them that couldn't help themselves she would—and she did.

"'I s'pose Maria has gone home,' says I to Luella, when I had gone in and sat down opposite her.

"'Yes, Maria went half an hour ago, after she had got supper and washed the dishes,' says Luella, in her pretty way.

"'I suppose she has got a lot of work to do in her own house tonight,' says I, kind of **bitter**, but that was all thrown away on Luella Miller. It seemed to her right that other folks that wa'n't any better

fortnight *(noun)* two weeks time

beholden *(adjective)* obligated

able than she was herself should wait on her, and she couldn't get it through her head that anybody should think it WA'N'T right.

"'Yes,' says Luella, real sweet and pretty, 'yes, she said she had to do her washin' to-night. She has let it go for a **fortnight** along of comin' over here.'

"'Why don't she stay home and do her washin' instead of comin' over here and doin' YOUR work, when you are just as well able, and enough sight more so, than she is to do it?' says I.

"Then Luella she looked at me like a baby who has a rattle shook at it. She sort of laughed as innocent as you please. 'Oh, I can't do the work myself, Miss Anderson,' says she. 'I never did. Maria HAS to do it.'

"Then I spoke out: 'Has to do it I' says I. 'Has to do it!' She don't have to do it, either. Maria Brown has her own home and enough to live on. She ain't **beholden** to you to come over here and slave for you and kill herself.'

"Luella she jest set and stared at me for all the world like a doll-baby that was so abused that it was comin' to life.

"'Yes,' says I, 'she's killin' herself. She's goin' to

pretty *(adverb)* partly; moderately

flame[ing] *(verb)* to glow; to blaze

die just the way Erastus did, and Lily, and your Aunt Abby. You're killin' her jest as you did them. I don't know what there is about you, but you seem to bring a curse,' says I. 'You kill everybody that is fool enough to care anythin' about you and do for you.'

"She stared at me and she was **pretty** pale.

"'And Maria ain't the only one you're goin' to kill,' says I. 'You're goin' to kill Doctor Malcom before you're done with him.'

"Then a red color came **flamin'** all over her face. 'I ain't goin' to kill him, either,' says she, and she begun to cry.

"'Yes, you BE!' says I. Then I spoke as I had never spoke before. You see, I felt it on account of Erastus. I told her that she hadn't any business to think of another man after she'd been married to one that had died for her: that she was a dreadful woman; and she was, that's true enough, but sometimes I have wondered lately if she knew it—if she wa'n't like a baby with scissors in its hand cuttin' everybody without knowin' what it was doin'.

"Luella she kept gettin' paler and paler, and she never took her eyes off my face. There was

awhile *(adverb)* for a time

conscience *(noun)* a feeling of the difference between right and wrong

witchcraft *(noun)* magic

offish *(adjective)* distant

somethin' awful about the way she looked at me and never spoke one word. After **awhile** I quit talkin' and I went home. I watched that night, but her lamp went out before nine o'clock, and when Doctor Malcom came drivin' past and sort of slowed up he see there wa'n't any light and he drove along. I saw her sort of shy out of meetin' the next Sunday, too, so he shouldn't go home with her, and I begun to think mebbe she did have some **conscience** after all. It was only a week after that that Maria Brown died—sort of sudden at the last, though everybody had seen it was comin'. Well, then there was a good deal of feelin' and pretty dark whispers. Folks said the days of **witchcraft** had come again, and they were pretty shy of Luella. She acted sort of **offish** to the Doctor and he didn't go there, and there wa'n't anybody to do anythin' for her. I don't know how she DID get along. I wouldn't go in there and offer to help her—not because I was afraid of dyin' like the rest, but I thought she was just as well able to do her own work as I was to do it for her, and I thought it was about time that she did it and stopped killin' other folks. But it wa'n't very long before folks

decline *(noun)* deterioration

bundle *(noun)* package
crawl *(verb)* to move slowly on hands and knees

nurse *(verb)* to help; to look after

set his eyes by her *(idiom)* admired her; looked
after her

spry *(adjective)* nimble; responsive

began to say that Luella herself was goin' into a **decline** jest the way her husband, and Lily, and Aunt Abby and the others had, and I saw myself that she looked pretty bad. I used to see her goin' past from the store with a **bundle** as if she could hardly **crawl**, but I remembered how Erastus used to wait and 'tend when he couldn't hardly put one foot before the other, and I didn't go out to help her.

"But at last one afternoon I saw the Doctor come drivin' up like mad with his medicine chest, and Mrs. Babbit came in after supper and said that Luella was real sick.

"'I'd offer to go in and **nurse** her,' says she, 'but I've got my children to consider, and mebbe it ain't true what they say, but it's queer how many folks that have done for her have died.'

"I didn't say anythin', but I considered how she had been Erastus's wife and how he had **set his eyes by her**, and I made up my mind to go in the next mornin', unless she was better, and see what I could do; but the next mornin' I see her at the window, and pretty soon she came steppin' out as **spry** as you please, and a little while afterward

caution *(noun)* a warning

poorly *(adjective)* sick; ill

wound up everything *(idiom)* concluded; ended

Mrs. Babbit came in and told me that the Doctor had got a girl from out of town, a Sarah Jones, to come there, and she said she was pretty sure that the Doctor was goin' to marry Luella.

"I saw him kiss her in the door that night myself, and I knew it was true. The woman came that afternoon, and the way she flew around was a **caution**. I don't believe Luella had swept since Maria died. She swept and dusted, and washed and ironed; wet clothes and dusters and carpets were flyin' over there all day, and every time Luella set her foot out when the Doctor wa'n't there there was that Sarah Jones helpin' of her up and down the steps, as if she hadn't learned to walk.

"Well, everybody knew that Luella and the Doctor were goin' to be married, but it wa'n't long before they began to talk about his lookin' so **poorly**, jest as they had about the others; and they talked about Sarah Jones, too.

"Well, the Doctor did die, and he wanted to be married first, so as to leave what little he had to Luella, but he died before the minister could get there, and Sarah Jones died a week afterward.

"Well, that **wound up everything** for Luella

earnest *(adverb)* to a serious degree

pitiful *(adjective)* causing pity or sympathetic
feelings toward

on account of [it] *(idiom)* as a result of something; because of something
done right by *(idiom)* to do what someone
would have wanted or expected

Miller. Not another soul in the whole town would lift a finger for her. There got to be a sort of panic. Then she began to droop in good **earnest**. She used to have to go to the store herself, for Mrs. Babbit was afraid to let Tommy go for her, and I've seen her goin' past and stoppin' every two or three steps to rest. Well, I stood it as long as I could, but one day I see her comin' with her arms full and stoppin' to lean against the Babbit fence, and I run out and took her bundles and carried them to her house. Then I went home and never spoke one word to her though she called after me dreadful kind of **pitiful**. Well, that night I was taken sick with a chill, and I was sick as I wanted to be for two weeks. Mrs. Babbit had seen me run out to help Luella and she came in and told me I was goin' to die **on account of it**. I didn't know whether I was or not, but I considered I had **done right by** Erastus's wife.

"That last two weeks Luella she had a dreadful hard time, I guess. She was pretty sick, and as near as I could make out nobody dared go near her. I don't know as she was really needin' anythin' very much, for there was enough to eat in her house

petted *(adjective)* pampered; coddled
done for *(idiom)* spoiled; coddled

duty *(noun)* required task

stopped short *(idiom)* to stop without finishing
juncture *(noun)* moment; a point in time
defiance *(noun)* contradiction; challenge

and it was warm weather, and she made out to cook a little flour gruel every day, I know, but I guess she had a hard time, she that had been so **petted** and **done for** all her life.

"When I got so I could go out, I went over there one morning. Mrs. Babbit had just come in to say she hadn't seen any smoke and she didn't know but it was somebody's **duty** to go in, but she couldn't help thinkin' of her children, and I got right up, though I hadn't been out of the house for two weeks, and I went in there, and Luella she was layin' on the bed, and she was dyin'.

"She lasted all that day and into the night. But I sat there after the new doctor had gone away. Nobody else dared to go there. It was about midnight that I left her for a minute to run home and get some medicine I had been takin', for I begun to feel rather bad.

"It was a full moon that night, and just as I started out of my door to cross the street back to Luella's, I **stopped short**, for I saw something."

Lydia Anderson at this **juncture** always said with a certain **defiance** that she did not expect to be believed, and then proceeded in a hushed

fairly *(adverb)* completely
midst *(noun)* the middle point

survived [her] *(idiom)* lived longer than
folklore *(noun)* a shared story that may not be
    verifiable

voice:

"I saw what I saw, and I know I saw it, and I will swear on my death bed that I saw it. I saw Luella Miller and Erastus Miller, and Lily, and Aunt Abby, and Maria, and the Doctor, and Sarah, all goin' out of her door, and all but Luella shone white in the moonlight, and they were all helpin' her along till she seemed to fairly fly in the midst of them. Then it all disappeared. I stood a minute with my heart poundin', then I went over there. I thought of goin' for Mrs. Babbit, but I thought she'd be afraid. So I went alone, though I knew what had happened. Luella was layin' real peaceful, dead on her bed."

This was the story that the old woman, Lydia Anderson, told, but the sequel was told by the people who survived her, and this is the tale which has become folklore in the village.

Lydia Anderson died when she was eighty-seven. She had continued wonderfully hale and hearty for one of her years until about two weeks before her death.

One bright moonlight evening she was sitting beside a window in her parlor when she made a

exclamation *(noun)* a loud and sudden
   statement

deserted *(adjective)* abandoned; left alone

helpless *(adjective)* unprotected; defenseless

emblematic *(adjective)* symbolic

sudden **exclamation**, and was out of the house and across the street before the neighbor who was taking care of her could stop her. She followed as fast as possible and found Lydia Anderson stretched on the ground before the door of Luella Miller's **deserted** house, and she was quite dead.

The next night there was a red gleam of fire across the moonlight and the old house of Luella Miller was burned to the ground. Nothing is now left of it except a few old cellar stones and a lilac bush, and in summer a **helpless** trail of morning glories among the weeds, which might be considered **emblematic** of Luella herself.

Notes:

NOTES:

NOTES:

NOTES:

NOTES: